"A Life Worth L

Charting Your Course
Directions for Real Life

Ross Brodfuehrer

COLLEGE PRESS
PUBLISHING COMPANY
Joplin, Missouri

Charting Your Course
Directions for Real Life

Ross Brodfuehrer

Copyright © 1999
College Press Publishing Company

Printed and Bound in the
United States of America
All Rights Reserved

Cover and internal layout designed by Mark A. Cole

All Scripture quotations, unless indicated, are taken from
THE HOLY BIBLE: NEW INTERNATIONAL VERSION®.
Copyright © 1973, 1978, 1984 by International Bible Society.
Used by permission of Zondervan Publishing House.
All rights reserved.

International Standard Book Number (ISBN): 0-89900-836-4

TO THE READER

A ship's captain has one main job.
 Stay on course.
 Then he can arrive safely and bring the ship home.

To do so he must keep watch, study his charts, read the stars, and make constant course corrections. He can't set out from port, point the wheel once, then retire to other duties.

Strong currents, cross winds, unforeseen storms, floating debris, even other vessels can all influence his direction, nudging him imperceptibly off line, slowly spinning him in the opposite direction, or even battering his craft to the ocean bottom.
 His vigil must be continuous.

You are a captain.
 You captain your life.
Are you on course?
 Do you know your bearings?
  Have you identified your port of destiny?

This devotion is designed to help you find a daily compass reading.
 It will take effort.
  Captaining always does.
   But a crew of 24 hours awaits your daily orders.
   Which way will you steer them?
   Who will guide your ship?

Charting Your Course is uniquely designed to use 3 ways:

✢ For individual study — Use each day's study to jump-start your journey and deepen your relationship with God.

✢ For Sunday School Classes — After each member completes the studies at home, discuss each week's theme as a companion to your regular curriculum. This is especially helpful as a thought-provoking opener.

✢ For accountability/small groups — have accountability partners pray for the specific areas of growth targeted in each study and hold each other responsible for a daily meeting with the Lord.

Acknowledgments

Thanks to the crew who brought this lightweight vessel ashore.

Southeast Christian Church for allowing me to work on its crew, giving me my sea legs in Christ and letting me try my hand at mapping such daily devotions.

Deena Kuhl who had the dream, designed the boat and nailed the thing together. You deserve the captain's chair.

Holly Koebel Detrick, Ellen Wokensperg, Dottie Koebel and Nancy Beasey who adjusted the rigging by typing, proofing and editing. Double rations of thanks to you.

Debbie, who showed me how to raise my sails into the winds of God's love and lift my eyes to the star-filled sky of possibility. I'll always be your cabin boy.

WEEK 1
A LIFE WORTH LIVING
What Would You Die For?

When you feel lifeless, when you are down in the dumps, when the alarm clock sounds like a clank of a prison cell door closing you into another long and torturous day, when the sun comes up but never seems to shine, when the energy is gone but the task still looms ahead . . . where do you go for relief? Where do the struggling go for strength to carry on? Where do the apathetic go for fire? Where do the listless go for life?

Try to think of all the places, people, and powers that humans seek out to fill their cups. The writer's list of "The 10 Most Popular Places People Look for Life" is at the bottom of this column, but before you skip down, do some thinking on your own. Where do you think people look for zest, pizzazz, and meaning? Write your 10 ideas in the next minute.

1. _____
2. _____
3. _____
4. _____
5. _____
6. _____
7. _____
8. _____
9. _____
10. _____

Now look at this list:

1. A physical/romantic relationship
2. A professional position
3. A well-furnished house and wallet
4. A close-knit family
5. Sensual indulgence (food, sex, artificial stimulants)
6. Dieting, appearance, attire
7. Distractions, hobbies, sports
8. Church membership
9. Being in shape and fit
10. Music, meditation, relaxation

✓ Check those on both lists.
⓪ Circle those only you had down.
✱ Asterisk those that you often turn to when you need a little pick-me-up.

7

FOCUS: READ COLOSSIANS 1:3-4
"We always thank God, the Father of our Lord Jesus Christ, when we pray for you, because we have heard of your faith in Christ Jesus and of the love you have for all the saints."
Whom could you say this about? Thank God for them now.

Oftentimes, people don't have a life worth living because the life they are living isn't worth living! Be honest. What would you say you are living for? What's your life all about?
What's your motivation?
Your hope?
Your dreams?
What is your life centered on?
Could it be money?
Could it be raising your young children?
Could it be life to you is all about making everyone else happy with you and never disappointing anybody?

What's been motivating you lately?
What keeps you at your daily grindstone?
Do you know?
If so, put your answer below. If you don't know, ask God to show you.

_____

_____

What does Paul pray that the Colossians will answer to that question? Read Colossians 1:9-10.
"For this reason, since the day we heard about you, we have not stopped praying for you and asking God to fill you with the knowledge of his will through all spiritual wisdom and understanding. And we pray this in order that you may live a life worthy of the Lord and may please him in every way: bearing fruit in every good work, growing in the knowledge of God."

_____

_____

_____

Would the things you have just written be worth living for?

❏ YOU BET!   ❏ NO, NOT ENOUGH!

How much is what you live for like the things Paul wanted these people to live for? Mark your answer on the continuum below.

NOT LIKE PAUL ⸻ **LIKE PAUL**

FIND LIFE BY DOING SOMETHING WORTH LIVING FOR

PRAYER: READ COLOSSIANS 1:11-14

Look at what God will do for someone living to please Him. "Being strengthened with all power according to his glorious might so that you may have great endurance and patience, and joyfully giving thanks to the Father, who has qualified you to share in the inheritance of the saints in the kingdom of light. For he has rescued us from the dominion of darkness and brought us into the kingdom of the Son he loves, in whom we have redemption, the forgiveness of sins."

FOCUS:
What did you do yesterday that was worth doing? Praise God for letting you take part in worthwhile things.

Here is a partial list of some influential leaders:

____ Julius Caesar		____ Buddha	
____ Moses		____ Mohammed	
____ Abraham Lincoln		____ Adolph Hitler	
____ Steven Spielberg		____ Princess Diana	

Which of these leaders were worth following and which were not? By each name put a (+) if a worthy leader, a (-) if a bad leader or a (?) if a questionable leader.

What leader have you primarily followed in life? More than anyone else, who has been your idol, your pattern, your influence?

____ father	____ mother
____ coach	____ friend
____ pastor	____ movie star/model
____ cartoon hero	____ teacher

His or her name _____

The leader we follow often determines our level of life. Write some of the qualities of a leader you have followed in the columns below.

_____   _____

_____   _____

_____   _____

NOW READ COLOSSIANS 1:15-23

"He is the image of the invisible God, the firstborn over all creation. For by him all things were created: things in heaven and on earth, visible and invisible, whether thrones or powers or rulers or authorities; all things were created by him and for him. He is before all things, and in him all things hold together. And he is the head of the body, the church; he is the beginning and the firstborn from among the dead, so that in everything he might have the supremacy. For God was pleased to have all his fullness dwell in him, and through him to reconcile to himself all things, whether things on earth or things in heaven, by making peace through his blood, shed on the cross.

"Once you were alienated from God and were enemies in your minds because of your evil behavior. But now he has reconciled you by Christ's physical body through death to present you holy in his sight, without blemish and free from accusation — if you continue in your faith, established and firm, not moved from the hope held out in the gospel. This is the gospel that you heard and that has been proclaimed to every creature under heaven, and of which I, Paul, have become a servant."

List some of the qualities of Jesus Christ below.

_____   _____
_____   _____
_____   _____
_____   _____

FIND LIFE BY LOVING SOMEONE WHO WOULD DIE FOR YOU

PRAYER:
Decide again whom you will follow in this life.

WEDNESDAY

FOCUS:
Father, who was my role model yesterday?

Suffering is a part of life. We suffer for something or someone almost every day. What we will suffer for largely determines whether we can find meaning and hope in that suffering.

Whom have you suffered for? A child, staying up night after night at her bedside during an extended illness? A boss who demanded 80 hours a week from you — and got it? A friend, who badly needed money, begged it off you, but never repaid as promised.

WHO_____

HOW_____

Answer these questions from Colossians 1:24–2:5.

"Now I rejoice in what was suffered for you, and I fill up in my flesh what is still lacking in regard to Christ's afflictions, for the sake of his body, which is the church. I have become its servant by the commission God gave me to present to you the Word of God in its fullness — the mystery that has been kept hidden for ages and generations, but is now disclosed to the saints. To them God has chosen to make known among the Gentiles the glorious riches of this mystery, which is Christ in you, the hope of glory.

We proclaim him, admonishing and teaching everyone with all wisdom, so that we may present everyone perfect in Christ. To this end I labor, struggling with all his energy, which so powerfully works in me.

I want you to know how much I am struggling for you and for those at Laodicea, and for all who have not met me personally. My purpose is that they may be encouraged in heart and united in love, so that they may have the full riches of complete understanding, in order that they may know the mystery of God, namely, Christ, in whom are hidden all the treasures of wisdom and knowledge. I tell you this so that no one may deceive you by fine-sounding arguments. For though I am absent from you in body, I am present with you in spirit and delight to see how orderly you are and how firm your faith in Christ is."

1. Who or what is Paul willing to suffer for?

_____

_____

2. What makes this worth suffering for?

_____

_____

3 Paul could write in v. 24, "I_____ in what was suffered . . . "

4. In your opinion, was Paul's suffering worth it and why. Before you answer, review his suffering in 2 Corinthians 11:24-29:

"Five times I received from the Jews the forty lashes minus one. Three times I was beaten with rods, once I was stoned, three times I was shipwrecked, I spent a night and a day in the open sea, I have been constantly on the move. I have been in danger from rivers, in danger from bandits, in danger from my own countrymen, in danger from Gentiles; in danger in the city, in danger in the country, in danger at sea; and in danger from false brothers. I have labored and toiled and have often gone without sleep; I have known hunger and thirst and have often gone without food; I have been cold and naked. Besides everything else, I face daily the pressure of my concern for all the churches. Who is weak, and I do not feel weak? Who is led into sin, and I do not inwardly burn?"

❏ YES   ❏ NO   ❏ UNSURE

Why?

_____

_____

_____

FIND LIFE BY LIVING FOR SOMEONE WORTH DYING FOR

Do this, and you will never suffer in vain.

PRAYER:
What else, who else, is worth living for and dying for, but you, Jesus?

THURSDAY

FOCUS:
What pressure, aggravation or suffering did you experience yesterday — and who or what was it for? Tell God about it.

Where can we get our power for life? One of two ways: a) from Jesus Christ or b) manufacture it ourselves. Read through Colossians 2:13-23 Contrast as you go what it is like to live by the worldly philosophy of trying to follow certain rules versus simply living in Christ.

"When you were dead in your sins and in the uncircumcision of your sinful nature, God made you alive with Christ. He forgave us all our sins, having canceled the written code, with its regulations, that was against us and that stood opposed to us: he took it away, nailing it to the cross. And having disarmed the powers and authorities, he made a public spectacle of them, triumphing over them by the cross.

Therefore do not let anyone judge you by what you eat or drink, or with regard to a religious festival, a New Moon celebration or a Sabbath day. These are a shadow of the things that were to come; the reality, however, is found in Christ. Do not let anyone who delights in false humility and the worship of angels disqualify you for the prize. Such a person goes into great detail about what he has seen, and his unspiritual mind puffs him up with idle notions. He has lost connection with the Head, from whom the whole body, supported and held together by its ligaments and sinews, grows as God causes it to grow.

Since you died with Christ to the basic principles of this world, why, as though you still belonged to it, do you submit to its rules: 'Do not handle! Do not taste! Do not touch!' These are all destined to perish with use, because they are based on human commands and teaching. Such regulations indeed have an appearance of wisdom, with their self-imposed worship, their false humility and their harsh treatment of the body, but they lack any value in restraining sensual indulgence."

Contrast as you go what it is like to live by the worldly philosophy of trying to follow certain rules versus simply living in Christ.

LIFE IN CHRIST	**LIFE ON YOUR OWN**

As Christians, we "live in Christ" (v. 6), He builds us and strengthens us (v. 7), and gives us His fullness (v. 10), and makes us alive (v. 13). What are the odds of your taking on the world on your own strength?

☐ 1:1   ☐ 50:1   ☐ 100:1   ☐ 1000:1   ☐ 1M:1

FIND LIFE BY ALLOWING CHRIST'S LIFE AND POWER TO WORK IN YOU

PRAYER: Jot some ideas down on how you could believe and expect Jesus Christ and His fullness to live through you today, rather than relying on yourself. Begin by allowing Him to work in you to answer this question.

▶ _____
▶ _____
▶ _____
▶ _____
▶ _____
▶ _____

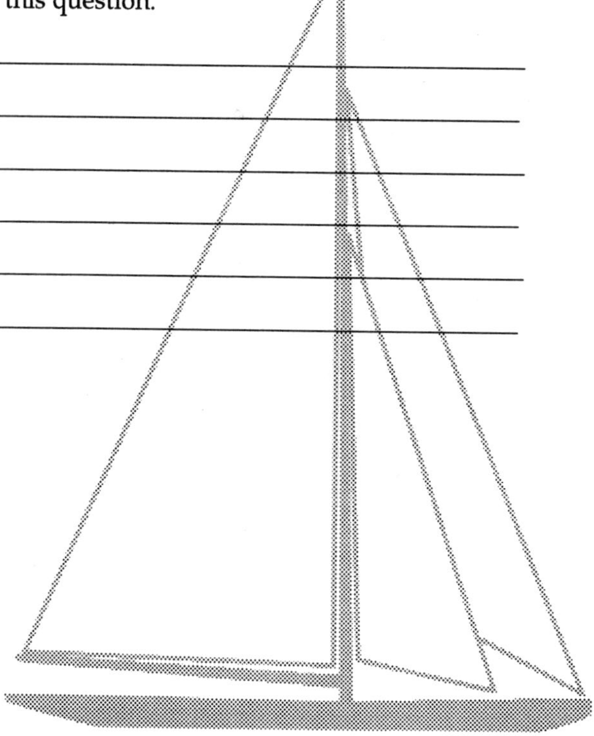

FOCUS:
What or who was your power source yesterday?

We all have enemies. The enemies may be people who dislike us, or even despise us. The enemies may be bad habits that drive us into stupid, destructive behaviors. The enemies may be physical disablers like disease or birth defects. Our enemies seek to trip us up and bring us down. Which enemies do you regularly face? Make a list.

_____   _____
_____   _____
_____   _____
_____   _____

For protection from enemies, some people buy a gun, others buy insurance; some double lock their doors, others double up on their exercise; some cross themselves while some double-cross others; some isolate, others retaliate; some duck out, others duke it out. What do you do for protection from each of your enemies listed above?

_____   _____
_____   _____
_____   _____
_____   _____

What enemies has Jesus defeated for you? Reread Colossians 2:13-23 from yesterday's devotions.

_____   _____
_____   _____
_____   _____
_____   _____

What power do we have to do what, according to 2 Corinthians 10:3-5 ?

"For though we live in the world, we do not wage war as the world does. The weapons we fight with are not the weapons of the world. On the contrary, they have divine power to demolish strongholds. We demolish argument and every pretension that sets itself up against the knowledge of God, and we take captive every thought to make it obedient to Christ."

Power:_____

To do what: _____
_____
_____
_____

FIND LIFE BY RELYING ON THE ONE WHO CAN DEFEAT YOUR ENEMIES

PRAYER:
Mighty Jesus, do I really believe You have the power and the desire to defeat my enemies? Do I live like it?

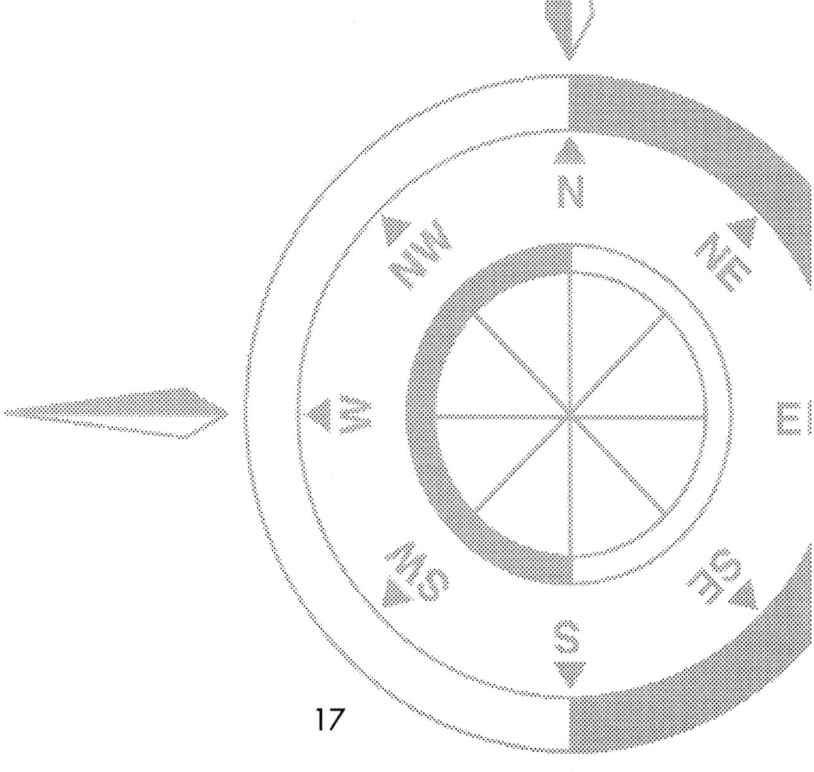

WEEK 2
ASKING THE HARD QUESTIONS
How Reliable Is the Bible?

What do you trust? Whom do you believe? *People* magazine? The *New York Times*? Your college textbook? The latest bestseller? Popular opinion?

The Bible has been around a long time, the "newest" parts having been penned 19 centuries ago. No writing compares to it, for it is undoubtedly the book with the most "mosts." Our Holy Bible is the most . . .

. . . widely read of all time. No other book has had more readers.

. . . published of all time. Its number of printed copies outdistances all competitors, as well as being the first ever printed on the Gutenberg press.

. . . translated of all time. It is now in every major language and most sublanguages.

. . . unique of all time. It was penned by 40 people of various occupations writing from three continents over 1,500 years in three languages, yet in astounding agreement.

. . . inspiring of all time. It has stirred more songs, movements, benevolent societies, schools, books, laws, paintings, plays, and individual transformation than any other book.

. . . quoted, criticized, examined, loved, hated, and believed book of all time. All types of people, from simple shepherds to sophisticated scientists, from African witch doctors to Wall Street wizards, from kindergarten kids to geriatric grandpas have accepted it as true.

. . . permanent of all time. It has outlasted Bible burnings, public ridicule, scholarly skepticism, and excommunication from our schools.

Jesus said, "Heaven and earth will pass away, but my words will never pass away."

MONDAY

FOCUS:
Pray as you study this lesson that you will see the truth.

You are on trial for forgery. You stand before the judge, who is vaguely familiar to you from childhood. The trial begins and your lawyer starts to make his opening argument. The judge stops him, and immediately pronounces sentence on you: guilty as charged. You protest: "Your Honor, how can you render a decision when you haven't heard all the evidence?" He replies, "Because I already know enough about you. I didn't trust you when we were children and I don't trust you now. Take him away!"

In this same haphazard way, many people have judged the Bible. Once the most revered book in the world, it is now one of the most scorned.

How capable are you of judgment? Do you know the defendant? If so, how well? Try this experiment: Open to your Bible's table of contents. List below all the individual books of the Bible that you have read from beginning to end.

Read Acts 17:10-12 The Bereans didn't swallow Paul's teaching whole hog, but they were willing to follow their heads over their impassioned prejudgments. Are you?
   "As soon as it was night, the brothers sent Paul and Silas away to Berea. On arriving there, they went to the Jewish synagogue. Now the Bereans were of more noble character than the Thessalonians, for they received the message with great eagerness and examined the Scriptures every day to see if what Paul said was true. Many of the Jews believed, as did also a number of prominent Greek women and many Greek men."

PRAYER:
Answer before God the questions in the third paragraph above.

 **FOCUS:**
Pray for an open heart.

What is claimed by the author in each passage below?

Jeremiah 1:4
"The Word of the LORD came to me, saying, 'Before I formed you in the womb I knew you, before you were born I set you apart; I appointed you as a prophet to the nations.'"

_____

_____

Ezekiel 1:1
"In the thirtieth year, in the fourth month on the fifth day, while I was among the exiles by the Kebar River, the heavens were opened and I saw visions of God."

_____

_____

Hosea 1:1
"The Word of the LORD that came to Hosea son of Beeri during the reigns of Uzziah, Jotham, Ahaz and Hezekiah, kings of Judah, and during the reign of Jeroboam son of Jehoash king of Israel."

_____

_____

Luke 1:1-4
"Many have undertaken to draw up an account of the things that have been fulfilled among us, just as they were handed down to us by those who from the first were eyewitnesses and servants of the Word. Therefore, since I myself have carefully investigated everything from the beginning, it seemed good also to me to write an

orderly account for you, most excellent Theophilus, so that you may know the certainty of the things you have been taught."

John 21:20-24

"Peter turned and saw that the disciple whom Jesus loved was following them. (This was the one who had leaned back against Jesus at the supper and had said, 'Lord, who is going to betray you?' When Peter saw him, he asked, 'Lord, what about him?'

"Jesus answered, 'If I want him to remain alive until I return, what is that to you? You must follow me.' Because of this, the rumor spread among the brothers that this disciple would not die. But Jesus did not say that he would not die; he only said, 'If I want him to remain alive until I return, what is that to you?'

"This is the disciple who testifies to these things and who wrote them down. We know that his testimony is true."

---

1 Corinthians 15:3-8

"For what I received I passed on to you as of first importance: that Christ died for our sins according to the Scriptures, that he was buried, that he was raised on the third day according to the Scriptures, and that he appeared to Peter, and then to the Twelve. After that, he appeared to more than five hundred of the brothers at the same time, most of whom are still living, though some have fallen asleep. Then he appeared to James, then to all the apostles, and last of all he appeared to me also, as to one abnormally born."

If you wrote a book, claiming it to be the very words of God, then you must be either:

- ⬥ making it all up (*lying*).
- ⬥ really believe it is true, even though it is not (*loony*).
- ⬥ telling the truth (*legitimate*).

The Bible is bursting with men and women who declare boldly that their words are true and divine. They held up honesty as a high value and taught the highest moral principles ever proclaimed in the history of ethics and religion. And their testimonies agree. Most times, the Bible writers' views were not Gallup Poll favorites. Many saints met with torture and execution for their claims, yet never reneged. How many liberal college professors, popular authors, and cocky newspaper columnists today would be willing to do the same? What would you state assuredly as the very Word of God? What beliefs are you ready to die for?

 **PRAYER:**
Thank God for spiritual mailmen who were willing to brave the storms, sleet, and snow of cultural rejection to give us the message of truth.

WEDNESDAY

 **FOCUS:**
Father, if your Word is true, help me to live like it!

The Scripture contains the loftiest standards and greatest moral truths of any writing — ever. Skim each of these passages and jot down one thing about it that impresses you.

Exodus 20:1-17
"And God spoke all these words:
"'I am the LORD your God, who brought you out of Egypt, out of the land of slavery. You shall have no other gods before me. You shall not make for yourself an idol in the form of anything in heaven above or on the earth beneath or in the waters below. You shall not bow down to them or worship them; for I, the LORD your God, am a jealous God, punishing the children for the sin of the fathers to the third and fourth generation of those who hate me, but showing love to a thousand generations of those who love me and keep my commandments. You shall not misuse the name of the LORD your God, for the LORD will not hold anyone guiltless who misuses His name. Remember the Sabbath day by keeping it holy. Six days you shall labor and do all your work, but the seventh day is a Sabbath to the LORD your God. On it you shall not do any work, neither you, nor your son or daughter, nor your manservant or maidservant, nor your animals, nor the alien within your gates. For in six days the LORD made the heavens and the earth, the sea, and all that is in them, but he rested on the seventh day. Therefore the LORD blessed the Sabbath day and made it holy. Honor your father and your mother, so that you may live long in the land the LORD your God is giving you. You shall not murder. You shall not commit adultery. You shall not steal. You shall not give false testimony against your neighbor. You shall not covet your neighbor's house. You shall not covet your neighbor's wife, or his manservant or maidservant, his ox or donkey, or anything that belongs to your neighbor.'
"When the people saw the thunder and lightning and heard the trumpet and saw the mountain in smoke, they trembled with fear. They stayed at a distance and said to Moses, 'Speak to us yourself and we will listen. But do not have God speak to us or we will die.'"

Deuteronomy 10:17-19

"For the Lord your God is God of gods and Lord of lords, the great God, mighty and awesome, who shows no partiality and accepts no bribes. He defends the cause of the fatherless and the widow, and loves the alien, giving him food and clothing. And you are to love those who are aliens, for you yourselves were aliens in Egypt."

Matthew 5:43-48, 7:12

"You have heard that it was said, 'Love your neighbor and hate your enemy.' But I tell you: Love your enemies and pray for those who persecute you, that you may be sons of your Father in heaven. He causes his sun to rise on the evil and the good, and sends rain on the righteous and the unrighteous. If you love those who love you, what reward will you get? Are not even the tax collectors doing that? And if you greet only your brothers, what are you doing more than others? Do not even pagans do that? Be perfect, therefore, as your heavenly Father is perfect. So in everything, do to others what you would have them do to you, for this sums up the Law and the Prophets."

John 3:16

"For God so loved the world that he gave his one and only Son, that whoever believes in him shall not perish but have eternal life."

1 Corinthians 13

"If I speak in the tongues of men and of angels, but have not love, I am only a resounding gong or a clanging cymbal. If I have the gift of prophecy and can fathom all mysteries and all knowledge, and if I have a faith that can move mountains, but have not love, I am nothing. If I give all I possess to the poor and surrender my body to the flames, but have not love, I gain nothing.

"Love is patient, love is kind. It does not envy, it does not boast, it is not proud. It is not rude, it is not self-seeking, it is not easily angered, it keeps no record of wrongs. Love does not delight in evil but rejoices with the truth. It always protects, always trusts, always hopes, always perseveres.

"Love never fails. But where there are prophecies, they will cease; where there are tongues, they will be stilled; where there is knowledge, it will pass away. For we know in part and we prophesy in part, but when perfection comes, the imperfect disappears. When I was a child, I talked like a child. When I became a man, I put childish ways behind me. Now we see but a poor reflection as in a mirror; then we shall see face to face. Now I know in part; then I shall know fully, even as I am fully known.

"And now these three remain: faith, hope and love. But the greatest of these is love."

Concepts, such as one God who is personal, all-powerful, and everlasting, originate in our Scripture. Other religions teach many gods, no god, or a cheap copy of the Judeo-Christian God.

Only the Bible takes sin seriously, pointing to its proper punishment of separation from a holy God, yet still tells of a God who loves, saves, and even sacrifices for His beloved creation. Other writings either downsize sin and concentrate on the achievement of personal fulfillment, or command man to make up for his own wrongs by good deeds. God remains distant, impersonal, or apathetic.

Only Christianity teaches putting others above yourself and loving even your enemy as a reflection of God's character. What a book!

 **PRAYER:**
If you didn't have the Bible, what would you believe? What would you pray?

THURSDAY

FOCUS:
Do I need to begin understanding God's guidelines?
God show me the truth.

What was the penalty for a false prophet according to Deuteronomy 18:20-22?

"'But a prophet who presumes to speak in my name anything I have not commanded him to say, or a prophet who speaks in the name of other gods, must be put to death.' You may say to yourselves, 'How can we know when a message has not been spoken by the LORD?' If what a prophet proclaims in the name of the LORD does not take place or come true, that is a message the LORD has not spoken. That prophet has spoken presumptuously. Do not be afraid of him."

Ouch! That could hurt. Even though the sentence was so severe, numerous deceiving prophets arose, telling people what "their itching ears wanted to hear." Often the true prophets were in the minority, while the "politically correct" prophets were rewarded.

Yet, only the true prophets' words held water over time, and so were preserved. Isaiah 52:13-53:12:

"See, my servant will act wisely; he will be raised and lifted up and highly exalted. Just as there were many who were appalled at him — his appearance was so disfigured beyond that of any man and his form marred beyond human likeness — so will he sprinkle many nations, and kings will shut their mouths because of him. For what they were not told, they will see, and what they have not heard, they will understand.

"Who has believed our message and to whom has the arm of the LORD been revealed? He grew up before him like a tender shoot, and like a root out of dry ground. He had no beauty or majesty to attract us to him, nothing in his appearance that we should desire him. He was despised and rejected by men, a man of sorrows, and familiar with suffering. Like one from whom men hide their faces he was despised, and we esteemed him not.

"Surely he took up our infirmities and carried our sorrows, yet we considered him stricken by God, smitten by him, and afflicted. But he was pierced for our transgressions, he was crushed for our iniquities; the punishment that brought us peace was upon him, and by his wounds we are healed. We all, like sheep, have gone astray, each of us has turned to his own way; and the LORD has laid on him the iniquity of us all.

"He was oppressed and afflicted, yet he did not open his mouth; he was led like a lamb to the slaughter, and as a sheep before her shearers is silent, so he did not open his mouth. By oppression and judgment he was taken away. And who can speak of his descendants? For he was cut off from the land of the living; for the transgression of my people he was stricken. He was assigned a grave with the wicked, and with the rich in his death, though he had done no violence, nor was any deceit in his mouth.

"Yet it was the LORD's will to crush him and cause him to suffer, and though the LORD makes his life a guilt offering, he will see his offspring and prolong his days, and the will of the LORD will prosper in his hand. After the suffering of his soul, he will see the light of life and be satisfied; by his knowledge my righteous servant will justify many, and he will bear their iniquities. Therefore I will give him a portion among the great, and he will divide the spoils with the strong, because he poured out his life unto death, and was numbered with the transgressors. For he bore the sin of many, and made intercession for the transgressors."

This is one prophetic passage for which Jewish scholars could find no convincing fulfillment until the coming of Christ. Note below any ways you see these verses being completed in Jesus.

_____

_____

_____

_____

_____

_____

Who else but Jesus mirrors these verses?

PRAYER:
Help me respond to this passage.

FOCUS:
Help me to take a step of faith.

One test of truth is the experiential proof. Does it jive with how things work; does it pan out? What does Jesus promise in John 7:14-17? "If anyone chooses _____, he will find out _____ _____."

In Jeremiah 29:13 God assures, *"You will seek me and find me when you seek me with all your heart."* One toe in the water doesn't do it; neither does an ankle, leg, waist, chest, or neck. It may be that the Bible commands baptism by immersion to demonstrate that we must go all the way in with the Lord. When a person abandons the baby end of the pool and trusts God enough to go to the deep end, the master lock is turned and the doors to understanding and enjoying God's pool begins. It all makes sense.

PRAYER:
Determine which sentence best describes you —

I trust and obey the Bible . . .

_____ not at all (out of the water).
_____ as much as it agrees with my common sense (baby pool).
_____ when it is easy (shallow end).
_____ fully and finally (the deep end).

WEEK 3
CHOOSING SIDES
What Is Christianity All About?

"Christianity is just another religion, not really any different than Islam, Buddhism, or Judaism. One believes in Mohammed, the other in Jesus, but they are all the same, except for some minor cosmetic differences that people like to fight about. The bottom line is: simply be good, love people, and you will get to heaven."

Is this your view? It shouldn't be! Christianity is unique and completely incompatible with any other religion. Buddhism teaches that man's goal is to escape the pain of personal existence in this world through right thinking. God's existence is secondary or denied. Hinduism teaches that there are many gods and many ways to "salvation." Their hope is also escape from conscious existence by becoming one with all that is. Islam teaches that by good works one can attain heaven.

Only Christianity has grace at the center. "God so loved . . ." Every other religion can be spelled with two letters: D-O. If you DO enough good deeds, pray the correct prayers, chant certain mystical chants, burn sufficient incense, detach from worldly stimulation, or die in a holy war, you can escape reincarnation, enter Nirvana, or earn a place in heaven. It is a matter of do!

Christianity can be spelled with four letters, the first two the same: D-O-N-E. God has DONE it for us by sentencing His Son to pay the price of our misdeeds. We, by faith, accept, not earn, His love and mercy. Christianity is an elevator, not the stairs; a gift, not a salary; a grant, not a loan; a full scholarship, not a work-study program.

MONDAY

FOCUS:
Lord, am I open to Your teaching this week? Do I really want to hear from You?

MAN IS CREATED WITH AN ABILITY TO CHOOSE GOOD OR EVIL . . . NO ONE ALWAYS CHOOSES THE GOOD

We make choices daily, hourly, by the minute, even by the second! Name three choices you have made in the last 24 hours (what you watched on TV, time you awoke, latest reading material, etc.).

1._____

2._____

3._____

What choice does Joshua give the people in Joshua 24:14-15?
 "Now fear the LORD and serve him with all faithfulness. Throw away the gods your forefathers worshiped beyond the River and in Egypt, and serve the LORD. But if serving the LORD seems undesirable to you, then choose for yourselves this day whom you will serve, whether the gods your forefathers served beyond the River, or the gods of the Amorites, in whose land you are living. But as for me and my household, we will serve the LORD."

_____

or

_____

Whenever you choose one thing, you are rejecting another thing. While many choices seem innocent enough, they are not necessarily so. When you choose to sleep in, you choose to shortchange God in prayer. When you decide to buy a new car, you decide not to give money away. Sin is not only doing what is obviously wrong, it can also be not doing what is right, or choosing something that is not very right, not loving, not God-centered.

What did Jesus say about His actions in John 6:38? ("For I have come down from heaven not to do my will but to do the will of him who sent me.")

_____

_____

 **PRAYER:**
Father, could I say what Jesus said about the three choices I made above? About all my other choices?

FOCUS:
Lord, whose will did I do yesterday?

THE CONSEQUENCE OF SIN IS SEPARATION FROM GOD

When in your life have your senses been close to God?

___ spiritual retreat	___ robbing a bank
___ mission trip	___ "one night stand"
___ in a worship service	___ at the bar
___ teaching children in church	___ telling a dirty joke

What do you learn from Isaiah 59:1-2?
   "Surely the arm of the LORD is not too short to save, nor his ear too dull to hear. But your iniquities have separated you from your God; your sins have hidden his face from you, so that he will not hear."

_____

_____

Separation. Divorce. Isolation. Alienation. Those are not our favorite words. They are lonely, painful terms. But since our God is "holy, holy, holy," He cannot tolerate what is "unholy, unholy, unholy," and oftentimes, that is us!

Like Adam and Eve, we choose the forbidden fruit and are ejected from God's presence, His paradise. The final separation is hell, excluded from all that is good, divine, loving, joyous, and meaningful; for outside of God, there is no good. Why do you choose sin when it separates you from the One who loves you most? Give an honest answer:

_____

_____

_____

_____

_____

_____

 **PRAYER:**
Confess your sin to Christ.

WEDNESDAY

FOCUS:
Jesus, have I been opening the door to You or closing it, walking with You or away from You?

GOD STILL LOVES US AND HOLDS OUT THE GIFT OF TRANSFORMATION THROUGH JESUS CHRIST

Write your name in each blank then read these words aloud!

God so loved _____ that He gave His one and only Son, that if _____ would believe in Him, _____ would not perish but have eternal life. God demonstrates His own love for _____ in this: While _____ was still a sinner, Christ died for _____. At one time _____ was foolish, disobedient, deceived and enslaved by all kinds of passions and pleasures. But when the kindness and love of God our Savior appeared, He saved _____, not because of righteous things _____ had done, but because of His mercy.

This is love: not that_____ loved God, but that God loved _____ and sent His Son as an atoning sacrifice for _____'s sins. (Based on John 3:16, Romans 5:8, Titus 3:3-5, and I John 4:10.)

Now read it again, inserting the name of someone you dearly love in the blanks. Insert the name of someone you dislike.

How have you seen God primarily? As a God of anger and punishment or a God of love and mercy? Who else can you name who has literally died for you, loved you when you didn't care, prepared a place for you to live for all time?

_____ I have fully accepted God's love.
_____ I have partially received His love.
_____ I have rejected God's love.

PRAYER:
Father, I will not further sin by denying Your favor on me. I receive Your love for me right now.

THURSDAY

FOCUS:
What difference did walking in the certainty of God's love for you make since yesterday's devotion?

WE RECEIVE LIFE TRANSFORMATION THROUGH FAITH IN JESUS

I know I have been accepted by Christ and will enter heaven when I die.

_____ Yes _____ No _____ Maybe

My hope of being right with God and entering heaven rests upon:

_____

_____

Put Ephesians 2:8-9 ("For it is by grace you have been saved, through faith — and this not from yourselves, it is the gift of God — not by works, so that no one can boast.") in your own words:

_____

_____

If a person truly believed this passage, what effects do you think it would have on his life?

_____

_____

Do you believe this passage? Have you opened this gift? What did the first Christians do to accept the forgiveness of God and the presence of the Holy Spirit? (Acts 2:37-41 — "When the people heard this, they were cut to the heart and said to Peter and the other apostles, 'Brothers, what shall we do?' Peter replied, 'Repent and be baptized, every one of you, in the name of Jesus Christ for the forgiveness of your sins. And you will receive the gift of the Holy Spirit. The promise is for you and your children and for all who are far off — for all whom the Lord our God will call.' With many other words he warned them; and he pleaded with them, 'Save yourselves from this corrupt generation.' Those who accepted his message were baptized, and about three thousand were added to their number that day.")

Check the statements you can agree with:

        _____ I know God loves me, despite me!
        _____ I know Christ died in my place!
        _____ I know it does not depend on me!
        _____ I know I am clean inside!
        _____ I know personal peace and joy!

PRAYER:
Commit to God to memorize Ephesians 2:8-9, then do it!

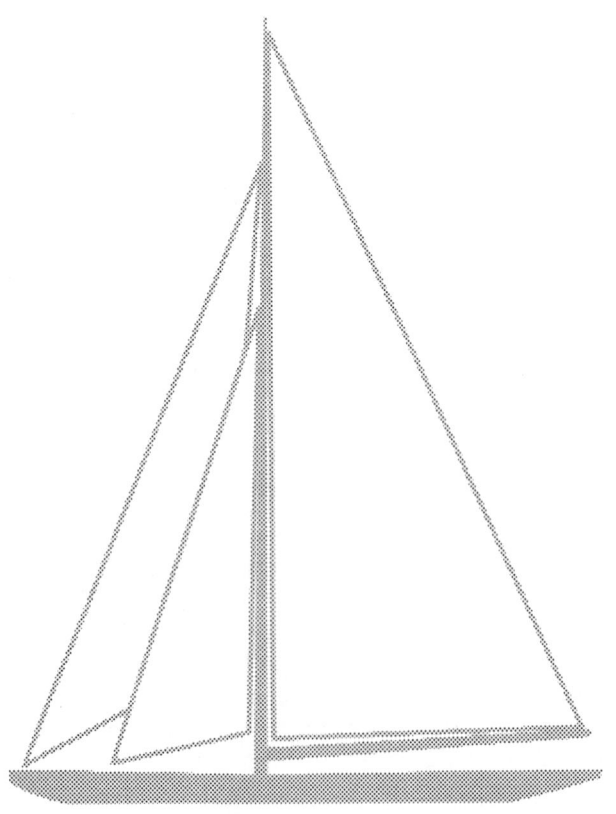

FRIDAY

FOCUS:
Gracious God, did I memorize Your words of grace? Did I live Your words of grace?

THOSE WHO SINCERELY BELIEVE ARE NEW CREATIONS AND DISPLAY IT IN THEIR ACTIONS

James wrote, "*I will show you my faith by what I do.*" What are some of the things a follower of Christ will be and do?

2 Corinthians 5:14-17

"For Christ's love compels us, because we are convinced that one died for all, and therefore all died. And he died for all, that those who live should no longer live for themselves but for him who died for them and was raised again. So from now on we regard no one from a worldly point of view. Though we once regarded Christ in this way, we do so no longer. Therefore, if anyone is in Christ, he is a new creation; the old has gone, the new has come!"

Galatians 5:22-23

"But the fruit of the Spirit is love, joy, peace, patience, kindness, godness, faithfulness, gentleness and self-control. Against such things there is no law."

(Circle) those actions/attitudes above that you can say you have done or are currently doing. Would a private eye sent to investigate your life find sufficient evidence to prove that Christ is in you and you are in Christ, new and improved?

_____ Yes _____ No _____ Hung Jury

If you are struggling for evidence, it could be that you are trying to live the Christian life untransformed — that is, by your own gumption and sweat rather than by God's free power. Read Ephesians 2:8-9, along with verse 10.

"For it is by grace you have been saved, through faith — and this not from yourselves, it is the gift of God — not by works, so that no one can boast. For we are God's workmanship, created in Christ Jesus to do good works, which God prepared in advance for us to do."

Whose craftsmanship should the believer be? His own or someone else's?"

PRAYER:
Father . . .

    ___ I rely on myself to live the Christian life.

    ___ I trust in Your power, grace, and joy to flow through me and do the things You have planned for me.

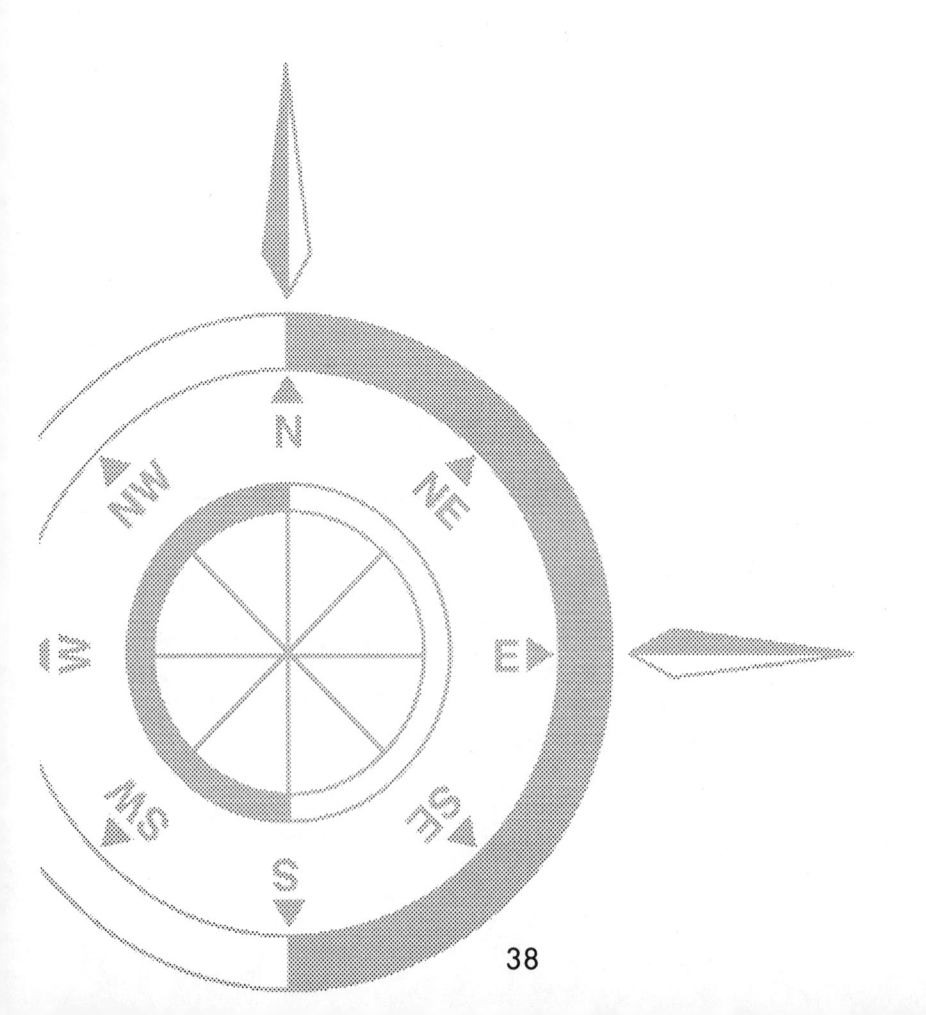

WEEK 4
IT'S YOUR MOVE
I Have Decided to Follow Jesus

"Come. Follow me!"

When you think about it, that's a presumptuous, impertinent invitation.

"Come, follow me" may not sound so haughty if one is simply saying, "Follow me to the nearest restaurant," or "Follow me as I show you how to use this computer program."

But "Follow me" as in "Go where I go, sleep where I sleep, do what I say, say what I say," now that's a bold invitation!

And if we add to it, "Leave your stuff behind: I'll take care of you; trust in me," that's ultra-dramatic.

It is even bolder when the one inviting is an unemployed day laborer with barely a red shekel to his name, no Ivy League diploma, no permanent street address, and a future littered with betrayal, ridicule, thorns and steel spikes.

"What do I get out of following you? What? No official title? No regular paycheck? No benefits? No company camel? No office on the 20th floor in the Jerusalem Towers? No end-of-the-year luxury cruise on the Mediterranean?

"What do I get? To be with you? Is that it? Oh, right. I also get to suffer with you! O boy! And a cross? That would be my favorite way to spend a Friday afternoon.

"I'll tell you what, let me think about this 'great' offer. I'll be in touch. (Yeah, right, I'll be in touch in your dreams, rabbi!)"

"Follow me."

Jesus did say it. He said it a lot. Daily. To everyone He met.

"Follow me."

Will you?

MONDAY

FOCUS:
What do you most like about Jesus Christ? Tell Him.

If you were going on vacation and could choose only one person to go with you, whom would you choose?

What if you were going on a mission trip to the jungles of Colombia, and could again have only one person go along, whom would you choose?

What if you had to take a dangerous military excursion to Iraq, then whom would you choose?

You are on a trip, a long trip that is part vacation, part mission, part combat. It's called life. What kind of person do you want guiding on this trip?

- ✧ Someone who can see ahead.
- ✧ Someone who knows the ropes.
- ✧ Someone who has great power.
- ✧ Someone who loves you dearly.
- ✧ Someone who knows how to enjoy life, be at peace, and live meaningfully.

Who meets these qualifications? Put Luke 7:11-23 in a nutshell.

"Soon afterward, Jesus went to a town called Nain, and his disciples and a large crowd went along with him. As he approached the town gate, a dead person was being carried out — the only son of his mother, and she was a widow. And a large crowd from the town was with her. When the Lord saw her, his heart went out to her and he said, 'Don't cry.'

"Then he went up and touched the coffin, and those carrying it stood still. He said, 'Young man, I say to you, get up!' The dead man sat up and began to talk, and Jesus gave him back to his mother.

"They were all filled with awe and praised God. 'A great prophet has appeared among us,' they said. 'God has come to help his people.' This news about Jesus spread throughout Judea and the surrounding country.

"John's disciples told him about all these things. Calling two of them, he sent them to the Lord to ask, 'Are you the one who was to come, or should we expect someone else?'

"When the men came to Jesus, they said, 'John the Baptist sent us to you to ask, "Are you the one who was to come, or should we expect someone else?"'

"At that very time Jesus cured many who had diseases, sicknesses and evil spirits, and gave sight to many who were blind. So he replied to the messengers, 'Go back and report to John what you have seen and heard: The blind receive sight, the lame walk, those who have leprosy are cured, the deaf hear, the dead are raised, and the good news is preached to the poor. Blessed is the man who does not fall away on account of me.'"

_____

_____

_____

_____

_____

Why wouldn't someone follow Jesus?

___ think Jesus is apathetic
___ think Jesus is away, absent
___ think Jesus is angry
___ think Jesus is unable
___ think Jesus is arduous
___ think Jesus is unappreciative

What would be your most likely reason for not following Jesus fully and finally?

_____

_____

TUESDAY

FOCUS:
Praise Jesus for the qualities you read about Him yesterday.

We studied yesterday just who would be a valuable companion to have walk with us through this journey called life. Today we look at who is worthy of our following. Besides our Lord, whom do you most admire?

_____

What are this person's outstanding characteristics?

▶ _____
▶ _____
▶ _____
▶ _____
▶ _____
▶ _____

List some of Jesus' outstanding characteristics. Allow Luke 23:26-49 to prompt your thinking.

"As they led Him away, they seized Simon from Cyrene, who was on his way in from the country, and put the cross on him and made him carry it behind Jesus. A large number of people followed him, including women who mourned and wailed for him. Jesus turned and said to them, 'Daughters of Jerusalem, do not weep for me; weep for yourselves and for your children. For the time will come when you will say, "Blessed are the barren women, the wombs that never bore and the breasts that never nursed!" Then "they will say to the mountains, 'Fall on us!' and to the hills, 'Cover us!'" For if men do these things when the tree is green, what will happen when it is dry?'

"Two other men, both criminals, were also led out with him to be executed. When they came to the place called the Skull, there they crucified him, along with the criminals — one on his right, the other on his left. Jesus said, 'Father, forgive them, for they do not know that they are doing.' And they divided up his clothes by casting lots.

"The people stood watching, and the rulers even sneered at him. They said, 'He saved others; let him save himself if he is the Christ of God, the Chosen One.' The soldiers also came up and mocked him. They offered him wine vinegar and said, 'If you are the King of the Jews, save yourself.'

"There was a written notice above him, which read: THIS IS THE KING OF THE JEWS.

"One of the criminals who hung there hurled insults at him: 'Aren't you the Christ? Save yourself and us!'

"But the other criminal rebuked him. 'Don't you fear God,' he said, 'since you are under the same sentence? We are punished justly, for we are getting what our deeds deserve. But this man has done nothing wrong.'

"Then he said, 'Jesus, remember me when you come into your kingdom.' Jesus answered him, 'I tell you the truth, today you will be with me in paradise.'

"It was now about the sixth hour, and darkness came over the whole land until the ninth hour, for the sun stopped shining. And the curtain of the temple was torn in two. Jesus called out with a loud voice, 'Father, into your hands I commit my spirit.' When he had said this, he breathed his last.

"The centurion, seeing what had happened, praised God and said, 'Surely this was a righteous man.' When all the people who had gathered to witness this sight saw what took place, they beat their breasts and went away. But all those who knew him, including the women who had followed him from Galilee, stood at a distance, watching these things."

▶ _____
▶ _____
▶ _____
▶ _____
▶ _____
▶ _____

Whom do you tend to mimic, pattern yourself after, want to be like or look like? Your father? A fashion model? A sports superstar? Your grandmother? A preacher? Is this person worthy of your imitation? Is he or she as worthy as our Lord?

Pledge yourself to mirroring the one and only perfect model, the only one worthy of your self-shaping.

WEDNESDAY

FOCUS:
Do you think you have praised the Lord Jesus enough the past two days? No way. Praise Him some more. Read Revelation 5 if you think we are overdoing the praise.

"Then I saw in the right hand of him who sat on the throne a scroll with writing on both sides and sealed with seven seals. And I saw a mighty angel proclaiming in a loud voice, 'Who is worthy to break the seals and open the scroll?' But no one in heaven or on earth or under the earth could open the scroll or even look inside it. I wept and wept because no one was found who was worthy to open the scroll or look inside. Then one of the elders said to me, 'Do not weep! See, the Lion of the tribe of Judah, the Root of David, has triumphed. He is able to open the scroll and its seven seals.'

"Then I saw a Lamb, looking as if it had been slain, standing in the center of the throne, encircled by the four living creatures and the elders. He had seven horns and seven eyes, which are the seven spirits of God sent out into all the earth. He came and took the scroll from the right hand of him who sat on the throne. And when he had taken it, the four living creatures and the twenty-four elders fell down before the Lamb. Each one had a harp and they were holding golden bowls full of incense, which are the prayers of the saints. And they sang a new song: 'You are worthy to take the scroll and to open its seals, because you were slain, and with your blood you purchased men for God from every tribe and language and people and nation. You have made them to be a kingdom and priests to serve our God, and they will reign on the earth.'

"Then I looked and heard the voice of many angels, numbering thousands upon thousands, and ten thousand times ten thousand. They encircled the throne and the living creatures and the elders. In a loud voice they sang: 'Worthy is the Lamb, who was slain, to receive power and wealth and wisdom and strength and honor and glory and praise!'

"Then I heard every creature in heaven and on earth and under the earth and on the sea, and all that is in them, singing: 'To him who sits on the throne and to the Lamb be praise and honor and glory and power, for ever and ever!' The four living creatures said, 'Amen,' and the elders fell down and worshiped."

See if you can imagine yourself saying what the man says to Jesus in Luke 9:57?

"As they were walking along the road, a man said to him, 'I will follow you wherever you go.'"

___ couldn't say it honestly
___ could say it easily
___ would have to think about it some more

Notice the word "wherever." What does "wherever" mean? Where did Jesus usually go? Where did He ultimately go?

_____

_____

_____

Do you think the man understood the implications of his commitment?

❏ Yes   ❏ No

Explain your answer.

_____

_____

Contrast the invitation time at the end of your church service with Jesus' response to this man "coming forward" to commit himself (verse 58). We encourage people to come and accept Jesus as Lord and Savior. How would you characterize Jesus' reaction to this man?

"Jesus replied, 'Foxes have holes and birds of the air have nests, but the Son of Man has no place to lay his head.'"

_____

_____

_____

Why such a tough response to this interested man?

_____

_____

_____

Prayerfully consider what it means to follow Jesus.

THURSDAY

FOCUS:
Whom did you follow yesterday?

What did you determine it means to follow Jesus during yesterday's prayer time?

_____

_____

_____

Based on how you defined "following Jesus," can you say confidently, "I follow Jesus"? If not, what would you say?

"I _____ Jesus."

Jesus calls another man to follow him in Luke 9:59-60.

> "He said to another man, 'Follow me.' But the man replied, 'Lord, first let me go and bury my father.' Jesus said to him, 'Let the dead bury their own dead, but you go and proclaim the kingdom of God.'"

What is your reaction to these two verses?

_____

_____

_____

The man's father may or may not have been dead already. He may have been saying, "My father's getting up in years; I'll follow as soon as he dies and the estate is settled." Or his father may have just passed away.

Either way, let the dead bury the dead. What do you think this means?

 ___ Let those in the graves come out and bury the deceased.

 ___ Let the spiritually dead, those senseless to God's presence, take care of such uneternal things.

Jesus was only on earth for a short period, publicly ministering for only about three years — three years out of the several thousand years of human history. If Jesus offered you just one day in the company of His physical, bodily form, what would you drop in order to go? What wouldn't you miss?

_____

_____

_____

Meditate on Luke 14:25-27.
"Large crowds were traveling with Jesus, and turning to them he said: 'If anyone comes to me and does not hate his father and mother, his wife and children, his brothers and sisters — yes, even his own life — he cannot be my disciple. And anyone who does not carry his cross and follow me cannot be my disciple.'"

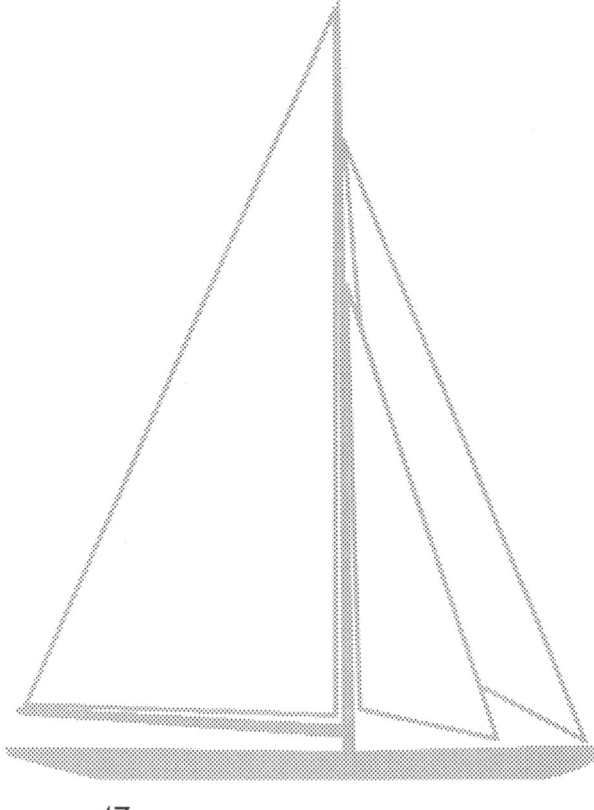

FRIDAY

FOCUS:
Lord Jesus, I love and desire you more than silver or gold, my mother, my dad, my spouse, my children, even my life.

The man in Luke 9:59-60 was exhorted to "let the dead bury their own dead."

"He said to another man, 'Follow me.' But the man replied, 'Lord, first let me go and bury my father.' Jesus said to him, 'Let the dead bury their own dead, but you go and proclaim the kingdom of God.'"

Jesus is saying, "There are plenty of spiritual corpses who can and will do the normal, earthly duties. Let them! Why don't you do the eternal, the earth-shattering, the Christ-glorifying things? Get out of the mud of the mundane, the dirt of the things of earth, and begin to do the eternal, the heavenly, the mountaintop things with me!" What do you think of Jesus for saying what He does in Luke 9:61-62?

"Still another said, 'I will follow you, Lord; but first let me go back and say good-by to my family.' Jesus replied, 'No one who puts his hand to the plow and looks back is fit for service in the kingdom of God.'"

_____

_____

_____

_____

You would think Jesus would be pleased with a man who will follow Him after a simple kiss goodbye to his wife and a hug for the kids.

But no. "Come NOW!" (Of course, the man might have been planning a more elaborate "good-bye party" lasting several days or weeks!) Do you find yourself saying, "Jesus, I'll follow you as soon as . . .

    . . . my wife is ready to follow.
    . . . I know more about the Bible.

. . . the house is paid off.
. . . I've succeeded in my business.
. . . the kids get through college.
. . . I retire.

Jesus is calling to you today. What is holding you back from following? What would He say to you about following Him?

"_____(your name), to truly follow me you must

_____

_____."

WEEK 5
EATING TOMATOES
Developing a Time of Quiet

Maybe you are thinking of starting a daily time of prayer and Bible study, but you have never done it before and don't know how.

Maybe a regular devotion time is one of your New Year's resolutions, but you have made resolutions before, and fallen on your face by February.

Maybe you have had a quiet time before, and it died a slow and boring death. You are afraid to try again because you don't want to fail again.

Maybe you have never desired more prayer. You don't like to pray. It's boring. But you now feel obligated as a Christian to read and pray.

Can a quiet time be meaningful? Interesting? Lasting? Life changing? Think about it this way: you may have hated tomatoes as a kid. Now you grow them in your backyard every summer and can't wait for them to ripen.

You may have never liked the opposite sex in elementary school, didn't want to even touch them. Now you go to sleep every night in your spouse's arms.

You may have avoided chores as a teenager, but now would rather tinker in the garage or do *anything* productive rather than slouch on the couch in front of another sitcom.

The things you love have changed with time and maturity. The Bible might be "tomatoes" to you now, but a year from now, it could be "TOMATOES!" Time alone with God may seem as unappealing as kissing your sister now, but as attractive as a holiday romance later. Getting up earlier may seem like drudgery now, but may become a joyful habit later.

Can it happen? You'll never know if you don't eat your tomatoes!

MONDAY

FOCUS:
Praise God for some of the good and perfect things He has given you: love, mountains, music, children, . . . Determine to believe that time with Him in private communion is at least as good as these!

Look closely at what God commands in 1 Peter 2:1.
"Therefore, rid yourselves of all malice and all deceit, hypocrisy, envy, and slander of every kind." Can you do what He commands?

```
___ impossible          ___ improbable
___ possible            ___ probable
           ___ likely
```

Maybe before you finalize your answer, you should note the use of "all" and "every" in this verse. It does not say rid yourself of "some," "most" or even "99 percent" of these. Nor does it say rid yourself of the worst kinds of malice or envy, but *every* kind.

Malice can mean hatred, scorn, dislike, wishing someone ill.

Deceit includes shading, hedging, hiding, puffing the truth.

Hypocrisy means trying to appear to be something you really are not.

Envy involves desiring other people's houses, talents, or spouses for your own; always wanting more.

Slander has to do with saying things behind someone's back you wouldn't say to their face, looking for occasions to spread dirt and whispering juicy gossip.

Now answer the question above again!

If you checked "impossible" or "improbable," remember Matthew 19:26:
"With man this is impossible, but with God all things are possible."
God specializes in the unlikely, and He illustrates it all around you. Tomorrow we will look at these divine examples. For now, can you believe that God can do anything, even rid you of all malice, deceit, hypocrisy, envy and slander?

51

TUESDAY

FOCUS:
Confess again, "God, I believe that with you all things are possible."

If you asked a small child if he thought he could ever read a 500-page book, pick Daddy up off the floor, or run a mile, most would say, "Oh no, I could never do that." And yet later, he does them all. When you were born . . .

- how much weight could you lift?
- how many words could you speak?
- how far could you walk?

How much of each can you do now? Are these abilities due to your constant training and tireless practice? Or are they due to God's miraculous life power given you at birth, a power that brought you from a microscopic blob to become a hearing, seeing, speaking, thinking, active agent in this world?

You are surrounded by examples of God's dynamic ability in turning little into much, one seed into a hundred and then a thousand, nothing into something, evil into good.

Just like at the feeding of the 5,000, Jesus can take your small loaves and fishes, and multiply!

Look at 1 Peter 2:2 and see what you are compared to in Scripture.
> "Like newborn babies, crave pure spiritual milk, so that by it you may grow up in your salvation."

As spiritual infants and toddlers, as most of us are, how much do you . . .

- know of the whole Bible? _____ %

- pray a day? _____ minutes out of 1440 minutes

- praise Him compared to the good He has done for you?
    None |————————————————| Fully

PRAYER:
How much can God multiply this in time?

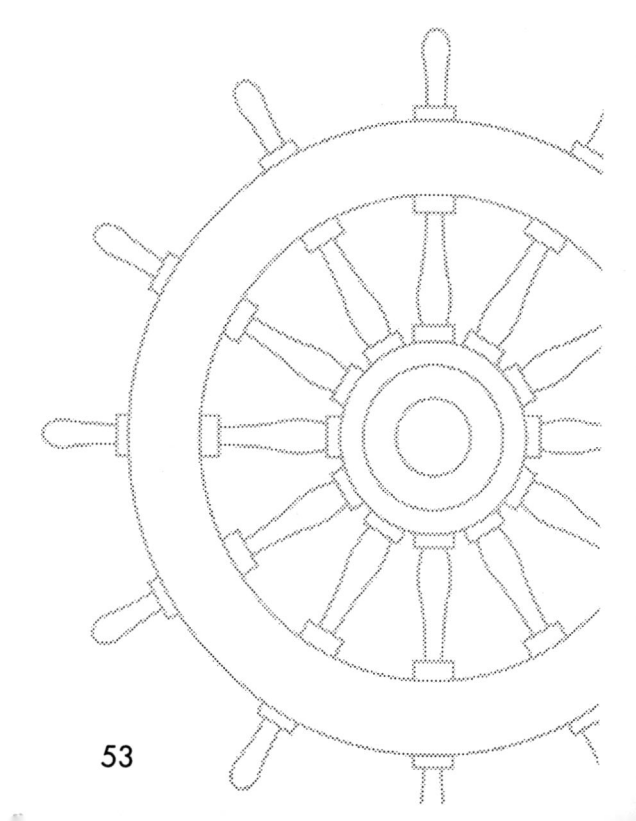

WEDNESDAY

FOCUS:
Thank God for the difference He has made in you since last year.

Picture yourself a year from now. What do you hope will be different?

_____

_____

_____

Five years from now?

_____

_____

_____

Thirty years from now?

_____

_____

_____

To reach these goals, it will take some changes! First Peter 2:2 says we should crave God's spiritual milk. What do you crave? What do you yearn for most?

❑ chocolate   ❑ sex   ❑ new clothes
❑ to win no matter what   ❑ peace in your home
❑ other _____

See if you can honestly pray Psalm 63. Don't move on until you have done this.

"O God, you are my God, earnestly I seek you; my soul thirsts for you, my body longs for you, in a dry and weary land where there is no water. I have seen you in the sanctuary and beheld your power and your glory. Because your love is better than life, my lips will glorify you. I will praise you as long as I live, and in your name I will lift up my hands. My soul will be satisfied as with the richest of foods; with singing lips my mouth will praise you. On my bed I remember you; I think of you through the watches of the night. Because you are my help, I sing in the shadow of your wings. My soul clings to you; your right hand upholds me. They who seek my life will be destroyed; they will go down to the depths of the earth. They will be given over to the sword and become food for jackals. But the king will rejoice in God; all who swear by God's name will praise Him, while the mouths of liars will be silenced."

What is your reaction to trying to pray this prayer?

_____

_____

_____

We often crave what will not satisfy. Think: when you are stressed, hurting, tired, mad, afraid, or lonely, where do you go for relief?

- ❏ phone a friend
- ❏ watch TV
- ❏ take pills
- ❏ do housework
- ❏ cry
- ❏ eat
- ❏ sleep
- ❏ drink
- ❏ mope
- ❏ shop

Are these things effective? Do they really solve your problems?

THURSDAY

FOCUS:
Make today a special day. Decide to give God some quality time. Crave his presence. Thirst for an audience with the Almighty.

Go back to Psalm 63. Use it as a guide to begin your conversation with the Father.

"O God, you are my God, earnestly I seek you; my soul thirsts for you, my body longs for you, in a dry and weary land where there is no water. I have seen you in the sanctuary and beheld your power and your glory. Because your love is better than life, my lips will glorify you. I will praise you as long as I live, and in your name I will lift up my hands. My soul will be satisfied as with the richest of foods; with singing lips my mouth will praise you. On my bed I remember you; I think of you through the watches of the night. Because you are my help, I sing in the shadow of your wings. My soul clings to you; your right hand upholds me. They who seek my life will be destroyed; they will go down to the depths of the earth. They will be given over to the sword and become food for jackals. But the king will rejoice in God; all who swear by God's name will praise Him, while the mouths of liars will be silenced."

Get on your knees and painfully confess your impurities, apathy, grudges, or any stumbling block between you and Him.

Thank Him for Jesus. Thank Him for the cross. For heaven. For life.

Cast on Him all your cares, problems, worries, family members, situations.

Believe He will respond.

Write below the results of your time.

Compare the results with the results you get from the other things you "crave," the things you normally seek to give you relief.

_____

_____

PRAYER:
End by reading Isaiah 55:1-2.

"Come, all you who are thirsty, come to the waters; and you who have no money, come, buy and eat! Come, buy wine and milk without money and without cost. Why spend money on that is not bread, and your labor on what does not satisfy? Listen, listen to me, and eat what is good, and your soul will delight in the richest of fare."

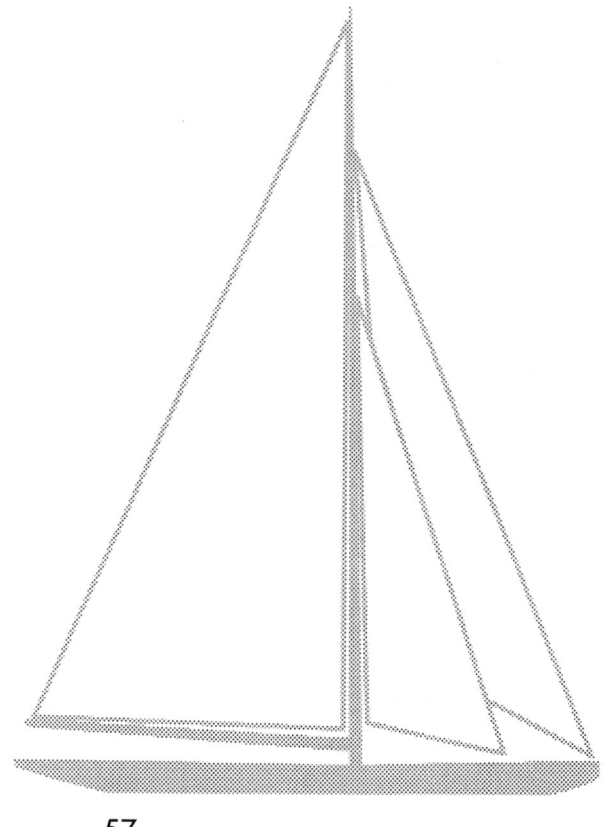

FRIDAY

FOCUS:
"I thirst."

Fill in the words to 1 Peter 2:3 ". . . now that you have _____ that the Lord is _____."

Has this been your experience with the Lord, that He is good? Or is time with Him as boring, tiresome, demanding and hard as ever?

Enrich your experience with God by doing different things with Him. When you first start dating someone, you do different things — a movie, dinner, a walk, a concert, stay up talking, visit relatives and so on. So it should be with God. You do different things with Him. You see Him in a different light. You draw closer.

Decide to try some of the following ways of knowing God better. Remember, though, these are not tasks to do, but a Person to meet; not a routine, but a relationship.

★ Do this devotion daily.
★ Take a walk and praise God for everything you see.
★ Give up one TV show a week and read a Christian book at that time.
★ Buy a praise tape; listen in the car every morning going to work.
★ Go to a weekly Bible study or join a small group.
★ Begin saying grace before meals.
★ Make a list of prayer requests; keep praying for them until they are all answered.
★ Try praying in various postures: standing, kneeling, lying prostrate, hands outstretched.
★ Try praying out loud.
★ Try writing a letter to Jesus.
★ Find a prayer partner.
★ Sing one praise song out loud to God each time you shower.
★ Make up your own ways to talk with, listen to, and spend time with your Lord God.

WEEK 6

DO YOU NEED SOME GOOD NEWS?
Jesus Came to Preach the Gospel

What would you consider good news? An unexpected bonus . . . your husband picks up his socks . . . your child is baptized . . . snow cancels school . . . sick in-laws can't come to visit . . . a promotion at work.

What some consider good news is actually bad news to others. A promotion may mean more pressure on the job or a move to another town. School snowed out may mean fun for the kids but a headache for a working single mother.

As far as good news goes, some is BIG good news (there is no sign of the expected cancer); some is medium good news (the cancer is operable); and some is small good news (we thought it was terminal, but with treatment, you might recover).

How do you see the Bible? Big good news? Medium good news? Small good news?

This listing may help you decide what you actually believe. Do you see the Bible as primarily . . .

- a law book of rules and penalties
- a get-well card
- marching orders for war
- a bonus check
- a road map for the good life
- a love letter

The Bible says Jesus came "preaching the gospel." Gospel literally means "good news." Make sure you have accepted it as good news for YOU as you study this week!

MONDAY

FOCUS:
Father, Jesus came to preach the Good News; help me come to learn the Good News.

How do you know what to do with your day? The options are countless. Sleep in. Do laundry. Pray. Go to work. Call your mother. Visit a sick friend. Play a game with your child. Eat out. Watch a soap opera. Clean the gutters. Read a novel. Study the Bible.

How do you choose? How did Jesus choose? Think of His options — and pressures!

- People needed healing — lepers, blind, deformed, dying people needed Him!
- People needed rescue — the iron boot of the Romans stood on the Jews' necks; taxes were out of sight; people were impoverished; fertile land was scarce.
- People needed challenge — religious leaders were two-faced and snooty, the people lowbrow and crass, sin rampant, love rare.

Jesus could heal, preach, erect a tent and have a revival, overthrow Rome, meditate on a mountain, write a book, start a school, or blow it all off and go back to heaven.

What would you have done?

List five things that Jesus did do, all in one day, in Mark 1:21-34.

"They came to Capernaum, and when the Sabbath came, Jesus went into the synagogue and began to teach. The people were amazed at his teaching, because he taught them as one who had authority, not as the teachers of the law. Just then a man in their synagogue who was possessed by an evil spirit cried out, 'What do you want with us, Jesus of Nazareth? Have you come to destroy us? I know who you are — the Holy One of God!' 'Be quiet!' said Jesus sternly. 'Come out of him!' The evil spirit shook the man violently and came out of him with a shriek.

"The people were all so amazed that they asked each other, 'What is this? A new teaching — and with authority! He even gives orders to evil spirits and they obey him.' News about him spread quickly over the whole region of Galilee.

"As soon as they left the synagogue, they went with James and John to the home of Simon and Andrew. Simon's mother-in-law was in bed with a fever, and they told Jesus about her. So he went to her, took her hand and helped her up. The fever left her and she began to wait on them.

"That evening after sunset the people brought to Jesus all the sick and demon-possessed. The whole town gathered at the door, and Jesus healed many who had various diseases. He also drove out many demons, but he would not let the demons speak because they knew who he was."

1. _____
2. _____
3. _____
4. _____
5. _____

How did He decide what to do this next day? Read Mark 1:35-39.

"Very early in the morning, while it was dark, Jesus got up, left the house and went off to a solitary place, where he prayed. Simon and his companions went to look for him, and when they found him, they exclaimed: 'Everyone is looking for you!' Jesus replied, 'Let us go somewhere else — to the nearby villages — so I can preach there also. That is why I have come.' So he traveled throughout Galilee, preaching in their synagogues and driving out demons.'"

_____

Was it what the others wanted Him to do? Was it the easiest thing to do?

What would have been the difficulties with this kind of lifestyle? Name three.

1. _____
2. _____
3. _____

PRAYER:
Thank Jesus for bringing good news, despite the obstacles.

TUESDAY

FOCUS:
Lord, what I think is good news is so often bad news in disguise. Clean my slate of my preconceived notions of what is and isn't Good News. Help me to be totally open to Your plan for my life.

The Bible is the story of people led by God to do what they did not expect and could not foresee. The convict Moses was called to free enslaved Israel. The shepherd David was called to be king. The uneducated Peter was called to be Jesus' right hand man. Paul, the perfect Jew, was called to travel the world to preach to Gentiles.

How do you decide what to do with your day?

_____

_____

How do you decide what is good news as you go through your day?

_____

_____

Look at Paul's conversion and call in Acts 9:1-19 and decide.
"Meanwhile, Saul was still breathing out murderous threats against the Lords' disciples. He went to the high priest and asked him for letters to the synagogues in Damascus, so that if he found any there who belonged to the Way, whether men or women, he might take them as prisoners to Jerusalem. As he neared Damascus on his journey, suddenly a light from heaven flashed around him. He fell to the ground and heard a voice say to him, 'Saul, Saul, why do you persecute me?

"'Who are you, Lord?' Saul asked.

"'I am Jesus, whom you are persecuting,' he replied. 'Now get up and go into the city, and you will be told what you must do.'

"The men traveling with Saul stood there speechless; they heard the sound but did not see anyone. Saul got up from the ground, but when he opened his eyes he could see nothing. So they led him by the hand into Damascus. For three days he was blind, and did not eat or drink anything.

"In Damascus, there was a disciple named Ananias. The Lord called to him in a vision, 'Ananias!'

"'Yes, Lord,' he answered.

"The Lord told him, 'Go to the house of Judas on Straight Street and ask for a man from Tarsus named Saul, for he is praying. In a vision he has seen a man named Ananias come and place his hands on him to restore his sight.'

"'Lord,' Ananias answered, 'I have heard many reports about this man and all the harm he has done to your saints in Jerusalem. And he has come here with authority from the chief priests to arrest all who call on your name.'

"But the Lord said to Ananais, 'Go! This man is my chosen instrument to carry my name before the Gentiles and their kings and before the people of Israel. I will show him how much he must suffer for my name.'

"Then Ananias went to the house and entered it. Placing his hands on Saul, he said, 'Brother Saul, the Lord — Jesus, who appeared to you on the road as you were coming here — has sent me so that you may see again and be filled with the Holy Spirit.' Immediately, something like scales fell from Saul's eyes, and he could see again. He got up and was baptized, and after taking some food, he regained his strength."

Was this really good news to Paul? What might make it seem like bad news — hard or difficult?

The Christian life is not easy, but it is easier than the worldly life. It does not appear so, but it is. And it takes faith to see it. Jesus said, "Come to me all you who are weary and burdened . . . . For my yoke is easy and my burden is light" (Matthew 11:28,30).

Do you think Moses, if he could, would go back and trade his 40 years leading Israel for a "normal" nomad's life? Do you think David wished he'd stayed with his sheep? Do you think Peter wished he'd never left fishing?

What are you staying with in your life — the "easy" worldly way, or the harder way of God's call, where real ease and life is to be found?

PRAYER:
Talk it over with God. "Lord, _____

_____

_____

_____

_____ "

WEDNESDAY

FOCUS:
What would you say the "good news" was?

Scripture always interprets Scripture. Jesus tells us what the news is in Mark 1:15. "The kingdom of God is near," literally, "the rule of God, the power of God's will to be done, is near."

That rule or power was not a thing or event, but a person. Jesus IS the ruler of God, the power of God, the will of God.

Where Jesus is, God's way reigns. And Jesus has come on the scene!

How do you see God's rule and way being worked out in Jesus through Mark, chapter 2?

"A few days later, when Jesus again entered Capernaum, the people heard that he had come home. So many gathered that there was no room left, not even outside the door, and he preached the word to them. Some men came, bringing to him a paralytic, carried by four of them. Since they could not get him to Jesus because of the crowd, they made an opening in the roof above Jesus and, after digging through it, lowered the mat the paralyzed man was lying on. When Jesus saw their faith, he said to the paralytic, 'Son, your sins are forgiven.'

"Now some teachers of the law were sitting there, thinking to themselves, 'Why does this fellow talk like that? He's blaspheming! Who can forgive sins but God alone?'

"Immediately Jesus knew in his spirit that this was what they were thinking in their hearts, and he said to them, 'Why are you thinking these things? Which is easier: to say to the paralytic, "Your sins are forgiven," or to say, "Get up, take your mat and walk"? But that you may know that the Son of Man has authority on earth to forgive sins . . .' He said to the paralytic, 'I tell you, get up, take your mat and go home.' He got up, took his mat and walked out in full view of them all. This amazed everyone, and they praised God, saying, 'We have never seen anything like this!'

"Once again Jesus went out beside the lake. A large crowd came to him, and he began to teach them. As he walked along, he saw Levi son of Alphaeus sitting at the tax collector's booth. 'Follow me,' Jesus told him, and Levi got up and followed him.

"While Jesus was having dinner at Levi's house, many tax collectors and 'sinners' were eating with him and his disciples, for there were many who followed him. When the teachers of the law who were Pharisees saw him eating with the 'sinners' and tax collectors, they asked his disciples: 'Why does he eat with tax collectors and "sinners"?'

"On hearing this, Jesus said to them, 'It is not the healthy who need a doctor, but the sick. I have not come to call the righteous, but sinners.'

"Now John's disciples and the Pharisees were fasting. Some people came and asked Jesus, 'How is it that John's disciples and the disciples of the Pharisees are fasting, but yours are not?'

"Jesus answered, 'How can the guests of the bridegroom fast while he is with them? They cannot, so long as they have him with them. But the time will come when the bridegroom will be taken from them, and on that day they will fast.

"'No one sews a patch of unshrunk cloth on an old garment. If he does, the new piece will pull away from the old, making the tear worse. And no one pours new wine into old wineskins. If he does, the wine will burst the skins, and both the wine and the wineskins will be ruined. No, he pours new wine into new wineskins.'

"One Sabbath Jesus was going through the grainfields, and as his disciples walked along, they began to pick some heads of grain. The Pharisees said to him, 'Look, why are they doing what is unlawful on the Sabbath?'

"He answered, 'Have you never read what David did when he and his companions were hungry and in need? In the days of Abiathar the high priest, he entered the house of God and ate the consecrated bread, which is lawful only for priests to eat. And he also gave some to his companions.'

"Then he said to them, 'The Sabbath was made for man, not man for the Sabbath. So the Son of Man is Lord even of the Sabbath.'"

_____

_____

_____

_____

What does Jesus tell Levi in verse 14?

"As he walked along, he saw Levi son of Alphaeus sitting at the tax collector's booth. 'Follow me,' Jesus told him, and Levi got up and followed him."

___ Follow this new program
___ Follow this new book
___ Follow your conscience
___ Follow me

Which of the above are you following? What is the ruler of your life?

_____

Where do you see Jesus — and God's will, power, and rule — happening in your life right now?

_____

_____

_____

PRAYER:
Lord Jesus, You have come.
    Come into me!
        Rule in me!
Be power and love and forgiveness in me!

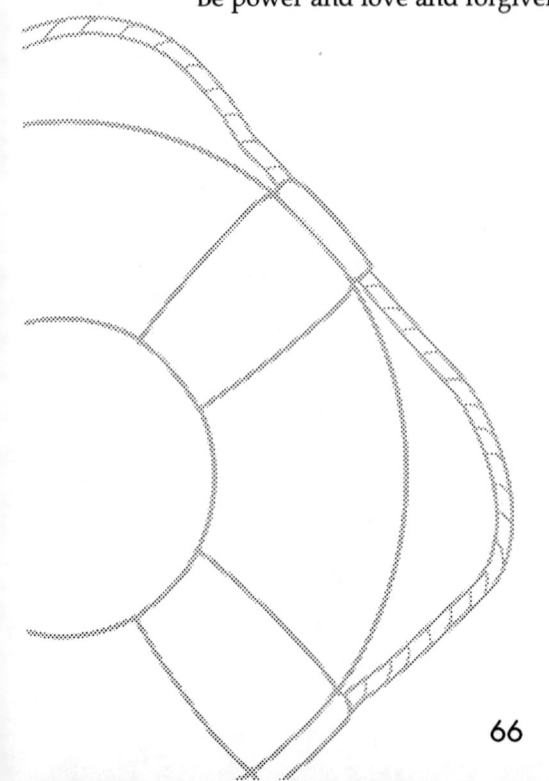

THURSDAY

FOCUS:
Thank Jesus for how He worked in your life yesterday.

No one who ever lived compares to Jesus Christ. Name any great leader, writer, doctor, teacher. None even comes up to Christ's knees! Buddha was an introspective seeker of self actualization; he never fed the hungry nor died for others. Mohammed did no miracles, healed no one; he killed, not raised the dead. Compare Jesus to Caesar, Michelangelo, Lincoln, Mao, Michael Jordan, even Mother Theresa! Christ stands alone in history. Jesus said that no one born of woman was greater than John the Baptist. If John was the greatest, how does he compare with Jesus in Mark 1:1-8?

"The beginning of the gospel about Jesus Christ, the Son of God. It is written in Isaiah the prophet: 'I will send my messenger ahead of you, who will prepare your way' — 'a voice of one calling in the desert, "Prepare the way for the Lord, make straight paths for him."' And so John came, baptizing in the desert region and preaching a baptism of repentance for the forgiveness of sins. The whole Judean countryside and all the people of Jerusalem went out to him. Confessing their sins, they were baptized by him in the Jordan River. John wore clothing made of camel's hair, with a leather belt around his waist, and he ate locusts and wild honey. And this was his message: 'After me will come one more powerful than I, the thongs of whose sandals I am not worthy to stoop down and untie. I baptize you with water, but he will baptize you with the Holy Spirit.'"

Jesus	John

Who are some of the great people in your life that you have admired and followed? Pick one to compare to Jesus.

Jesus	Your choice
loved all	
sinless	

healed the sick
raised the dead
forgave sin
died for others
rose from the dead

Now compare Jesus to YOU! How do you fare?

In John 17:26, Jesus said that He came so that "I myself may be in [my disciples]." He did not say, "So that a small part of me may be in them," but "I myself."
How will you welcome The Great One into your life again today?

PRAYER: "O holy child of Bethlehem, descend to us, we pray. Cast out our sin and enter in. Be born in us today."

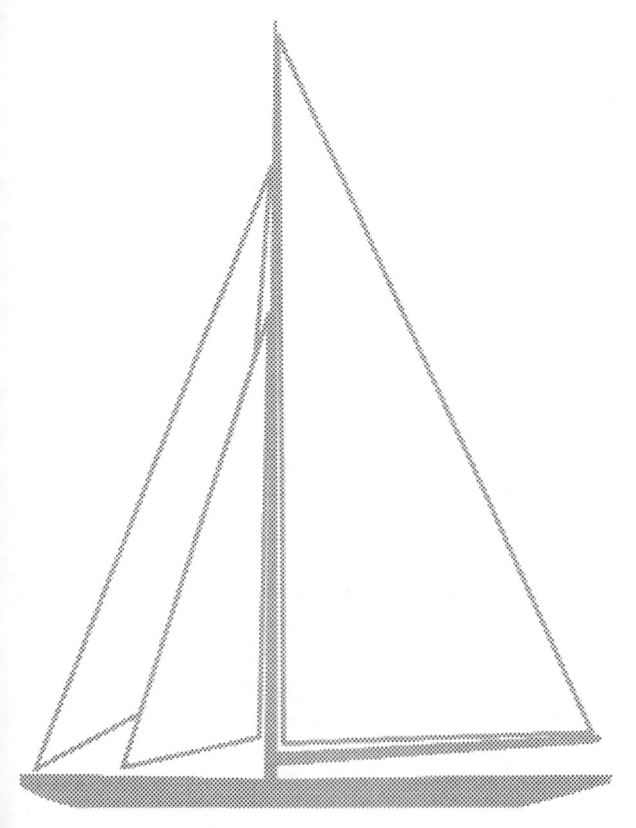

FRIDAY

FOCUS:
Talk over your yesterday with the BIG GOOD NEWS of your life, the person, Jesus Christ.

How do you react to good news? It probably depends on your personality. Which describes you upon hearing some good news?

    ___ That's nice. (straight face)
    ___ Good! (smile)
    ___ Great! (high fives)
    ___ Woooeee! (dancing and hugs)

Look at the people who received the Good News (Jesus Christ's very presence) in Mark, chapter 1, and describe how they reacted to Him.

Person(s)	**Reaction**

Read Mark 4:1-20 and decide which of the below you are.

"Again Jesus began to teach by the lake. The crowd that gathered around him was so large that he got into a boat and sat in it out on the lake, while all the people were along the shore at the water's edge. He taught them many things by parables, and in his teaching said: 'Listen! A farmer went out to sow his seed. As he was scattering the seed, some fell along the path, and the birds came and ate it up. Some fell on rocky places, where it did not have much soil. It sprang up quickly, because the soil was shallow. But when the sun came up, the plants were scorched, and they withered because they had no root. Other seed fell among thorns, which grew up and choked the plants, so that they did not bear grain. Still other seed fell on good soil. It came up, grew and produced a crop, multiplying thirty, sixty, or even a hundred times.'

"Then Jesus said, 'He who has ears to hear, let him hear.'

"When he was alone, the Twelve and the others around him asked him about the parables. He told them, 'The secret of the kingdom of God has been given to you. But to those on the outside everything is said in parables so that, "they may be ever seeing but never perceiving, and ever hearing but never understanding; otherwise they might turn and be forgiven!"'

"Then Jesus said to them, 'Don't you understand this parable? How then will you understand any parable? The farmer sows the word. Some people are like seed along the path, where the word is sown. As soon as they hear it, Satan comes and takes away the word that was sown in them. Others, like seed sown on rocky places, hear the word and at once receive it with joy. But since they have no root, they last only a short time. When trouble or persecution comes because of the word, they quickly fall away. Still others, like seed sown among thorns, hear the word; but the worries of this life, the deceitfulness of wealth and the desires for other things come in and choke the word, making it unfruitful. Others, like seed sown on good soil, hear the word, accept it, and produce a crop — thirty, sixty or even a hundred times what was sown.'"

___ path ___ rocky soil
___ thorny soil ___ good soil

What has Jesus' presence done in your life — not necessarily what you have done, but what the miracle worker has done in you? Mentally list as much "fruit" as you can. Use this space to write some of them down.

Which of the reactions you listed from Mark 1 do you have toward Jesus' presence in your life? Circle them.

PRAYER:
Express your appreciation to your Lord Jesus.

WEEK 7
FINDING YOUR WAY HOME
Jesus Came to Seek and Save the Lost

LOST . . .
      lost . . .
            lost.

What a lonely, echoing, terrifying word. LOST!

Do you remember the first time you were lost — maybe in a grocery store or in the woods behind your house. How did it feel?

Lost is a bad thing to be. But there are all kinds of "lostness."

- lost your way
- lost your hope
- lost your heart
- lost your cool
- lost your reputation
- lost your family
- lost your mind

A man may feel lost even in his own home — the once-loud rooms become caves of silence after the divorce.

A woman may feel lost when the children have all moved out and she no longer knows her purpose for living.

A businessman may feel lost when he has reached all his goals but is strangely empty and uneasy.

A boy may feel lost when he lies in the quiet of his bed at night and wonders if there is anyone who really cares about him.

Jesus came to SEEK and save the lost. He searches out the lost. He wants the lost. He calls to the lost.

Are you lost in any way? Or are you exactly sure where you are in this spinning world? Are you sure where you belong among your people? Sure where you stand with God above?

Come and be found!

MONDAY

FOCUS:
Pray for all those who will be doing this study, that any who are lost may be found.

JESUS CAME TO FIND THOSE WHO HAVE LOST THEIR PURITY

Read John 8:1-11.

"But Jesus went to the Mount of Olives. At dawn he appeared again in the temple courts, where all the people gathered around him, and he sat down to teach them. The teachers of the law and the Pharisees brought in a woman caught in adultery. They made her stand before the group and said to Jesus, 'Teacher, this woman was caught in the act of adultery. In the Law Moses commanded us to stone such women. Now what do you say?' They were using this question as a trap, in order to have a basis for accusing him.

"But Jesus bent down and started to write on the ground with His finger. When they kept on questioning him, he straightened up and said to them, 'If any one of you is without sin, let him be the first to throw a stone at her.' Again he stooped down and wrote on the ground.

"At this, those who heard began to go away one at a time, the older ones first, until only Jesus was left, with the woman still standing there. Jesus straightened up and asked her, 'Woman, where are they? Has no one condemned you?'

"'No one, sir,' she said.

"'Then neither do I condemn you,' Jesus declared. 'Go now and leave your life of sin.'"

Were people repulsed by Jesus or attracted to Him? _____

What was the religious leaders' intention in coming to Jesus?
_____
_____

How much did they care about the woman they brought to Jesus?
_____
_____

The Law does say that the adulterer must die (Leviticus 20:10).

> "'If a man commits adultery with another man's wife — with the wife of his neighbor — both the adulterer and the adulteress must be put to death.'"

Jesus said that not the least aspect of the Law should be neglected. What is the meaning of His verdict in verse 7?

_____

_____

Who had the right to condemn this woman, if only the sinless could do so? _____

The death penalty of the Law *was* fulfilled for this woman, though she did not die. Who did? _____

Has your sexual purity been lost? Take a short journey with this adulterous woman.

Who has accused you of being dirty, unworthy, unlovable?

_____   _____

_____   _____

Did they say this because they love you or to make themselves feel better?

❏ love me   ❏ make them feel better

Who alone has the right to condemn you or to pardon you?

_____

Can you hear Jesus say to you the words of verse 11?

PRAYER:
Lord Jesus, You desire to restore, not destroy; to mend, not mock; to purify, not prosecute. Help me to hear Your voice above all others, for the others are sinners just as I am. You alone may pass sentence — and you have in verse 11!

TUESDAY

FOCUS:
Who has lost heart around you? Pray for them.

JESUS CAME TO FIND THOSE WHO HAVE LOST HEART

Have you ever lost heart? Given up hope? Thrown in the towel?

Have others ever named you hopeless: "You'll always be a loser! You can never amount to anything."

2 Corinthians 4:16 says, "We do not lose heart." With Christ, there is no hopeless man or futureless woman. What descriptions are given of Zacchaeus in Luke 19:1-10?

"Jesus entered Jericho and was passing through. A man was there by the name of Zacchaeus; he was a chief tax collector and was wealthy. He wanted to see who Jesus was, but being a short man he could not, because of the crowd. So he ran ahead and climbed a sycamore-fig tree to see him, since Jesus was coming that way.

"When Jesus reached the spot, he looked up and said to him, 'Zacchaeus, come down immediately. I must stay at your house today.' So he came down at once and welcomed him gladly.

"All the people saw this and began to mutter, 'He has gone to be the guest of a "sinner."'

"But Zacchaues stood up and said to the Lord, 'Look, Lord! Here and now I give half of my possessions to the poor, and if I have cheated anybody out of anything, I will pay back four times the amount.'

"Jesus said to him, 'Today salvation has come to this house, because this man, too, is a son of Abraham. For the Son of Man came to seek and to save what was lost.'"

verse 2: _____

verse 3: _____

verse 7: _____

verse 9: _____

verse10: _____

Based on what Zacchaeus says in verse 8, do you think he was an honest tax collector?

❏ Yes ❏ No

Look again at how the people saw Zacchaeus in verse 7.

What percentage of the people saw him this way? _____ %

What characteristics do you most despise in others?

___ rich	___ poor
___ smart	___ dumb
___ skinny	___ fat
___ loud/pushy	___ shy/timid
___ pretty	___ ugly
___ pure	___ sinful

How did Jesus see this short, rich, cheating, hated tax collector?

_____
_____

Name a person you despise. _____ He/she is your Zacchaeus!
How does Jesus see this person? How should you see him/her?

_____
_____

PRAYER:
Lord Jesus, You came to find and save those we see as hopeless and worthless. Forgive me for being one of the condemners. Help me to join You in the search!

WEDNESDAY

FOCUS:
"Lord, I have strayed like a lost sheep. Seek your servant, for I have not forgotten your commands" (Psalm 119:176).

JESUS CAME TO FIND THOSE WHO HAVE LOST THEIR WAY

Remember the show *Lost in Space*? Every episode was an attempt by the Robinson family to get back on the right track to earth. Every show was also filled with tension, uncertainty, and frustrating failure.

We, too, can be lost in our spacious, busy world of limitless options, and be uncertain what to do next. We can be on edge, tense, uneasy. We're "lost in our own space." Contrast Jesus' life purpose with Peter's thinking in Matthew 16:21-28.

"From that time on Jesus began to explain to his disciples that he must go to Jerusalem and suffer many things at the hands of the elders, chief priests and teachers of the law, and that he must be killed and on the third day be raised to life.

"Peter took him aside and began to rebuke him. 'Never, Lord!' he said. 'This shall never happen to you!'

"Jesus turned and said to Peter, 'Get behind me, Satan! You are a stumbling block to me; you do not have in mind the things of God, but the things of men.'

"Then Jesus said to His disciples, 'If anyone would come after me, he must deny himself and take up his cross and follow me. For whoever wants to save his life will lose it, but whoever loses his life for me will find it. What good will it be for a man if he gains the whole world, yet forfeits his soul? For the Son of Man is going to come in his Father's glory with his angels, and then he will reward each person according to what he has done. I tell you the truth, some who are standing here will not taste death before they see the Son of Man coming in His kingdom.'"

Where do Peter's ideas come from?

"Get behind me, _____."

"You do not have in mind the things of God, but the things of _____."

Which philosophy of life is closer to yours?

___ Peter's   ___ Jesus'

List three decisions/actions you made this past week. Name anything.

1. _____
2. _____
3. _____

What was your primary criteria for deciding what you did?

- ☐ look good to others
- ☐ make the most money
- ☐ have fun
- ☐ avoid pain or hardship
- ☐ sense of duty or "have to"
- ☐ honor and serve Jesus

Could it be you feel lost because you have concentrated on finding yourself rather than on losing yourself for Jesus? If you have lived to find and save your life, what has it brought you?

PRAYER:
Father, help me not to be lured into the unsatisfying, self-serving rat race of this world. Today Jesus will be my only Way, my only Truth, my only Life.

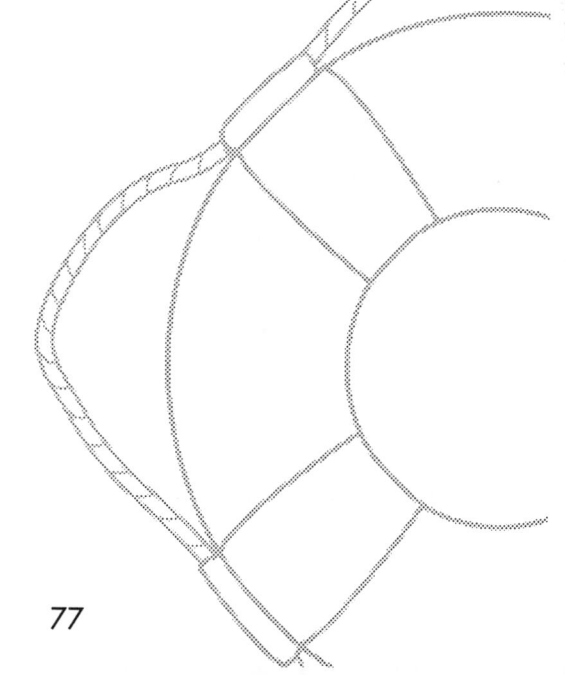

THURSDAY

FOCUS:
Thank you, Lord, for being a true father to me.

JESUS CAME TO FIND THOSE WHO HAVE LOST THEIR FATHER

Remember Peter Pan's Lost Boys? They had no family, no father. Did you have a father? Not just someone who sat in a chair, watched sports, drank beer and barked orders. Not someone who worked overtime to put bread on the table and presents under the Christmas tree. But a total dad who held you on his lap, read you bedtime stories, played and prayed with you. Describe your dad:

_____
_____
_____
_____

How did your dad make you feel? _____

The human personality is, for the most part, ingrained by the age of seven. Many of us have a fatherless personality, for even though he was present, our dad may not have known how to love. We are spiritual and emotional orphans. Underline the words or phrases that reflect Jesus' concern that children are found and loved in Matthew 18:5-14.

"And whoever welcomes a little child like this in my name welcomes me. But if anyone causes one of these little ones who believe in me to sin, it would be better for him to have a large millstone hung around his neck and to be drowned in the depths of the sea.

"Woe to the world because of the things that cause people to sin! Such things must come, but woe to the man through whom they come! If your hand or your foot causes you to sin, cut if off and throw it away. It is better for you to enter life maimed or crippled than to have two hands or two feet and be thrown into eternal fire. And if your eye causes you to sin, gouge it out and throw it away. It is better for you to enter life with one eye than to have two eyes and be thrown into the fire of hell.

"See that you do not look down on one of these little ones. For I tell you that their angels in heaven always see the face of my Father in heaven.

"What do you think? If a man owns a hundred sheep, and one of them wanders away, will he not leave the ninety-nine on the hills and go to look for the one that wandered off? And if he finds it, I tell you the truth, he is happier about that one sheep than about the ninety-nine that did not wander off. In the same way your Father in heaven is not willing that any of these little ones should be lost."

What does Jesus call God in this passage? _____

Jesus said, "Anyone who has seen me has seen the Father" (John 14:9). Read again the famous story of the prodigal son in Luke 15:11-32 and decide where you are in your relationship with your Father God:

❏ in the far country
❏ walking toward home
❏ seeing the Father running to you
❏ pleading His forgiveness
❏ accepting the ring, robe and sandals
❏ at the party in His house
❏ outside with the older brother.

PRAYER:
Use verses 21-27 as a guide for your prayer.

FRIDAY

FOCUS:
I love you, Lord, for You love to find the lost!

JESUS CAME TO FIND THOSE WHO HAVE LOST THEIR MINDS

Paul said we Christians "have the mind of Christ" (1 Corinthians 2:16). But we can have "unspiritual or corrupt minds" if Christ be not our mind. (Romans 12:2; Colossians 2:18; 1 Timothy 6:5)

Mark 5:1-20 is the story of a man not in his right mind. Actually, it is the story of several men not in their right minds, but we'll get to that later.

"They went across the lake to the region of the Gerasenes. When Jesus got out of the boat, a man with an evil spirit came from the tombs to meet him. This man lived in the tombs, and no one could bind him any more, not even with a chain. For he had often been chained hand and foot, but he tore the chains apart and broke the irons on his feet. No one was strong enough to subdue him. Night and day among the tombs and in the hills he would cry out and cut himself with stones.

"When he saw Jesus from a distance, he ran and fell on his knees in front of Him. He shouted at the top of his voice, 'What do you want with me, Jesus, Son of the Most High God? Swear to God that you won't torture me!' For Jesus had said to him, 'Come out of this man, you evil spirit!'

"Then Jesus asked him, 'What is your name?'

"'My name is Legion,' he replied, 'for we are many.' And he begged Jesus again and again not to send them out of the area.

"A large heard of pigs was feeding on the nearby hillside. The demons begged Jesus, 'Send us among the pigs; allow us to go into them.' He gave them permission, and the evil spirits came out and went into the pigs. The herd, about two thousand in number, rushed down the steep bank into the lake and were drowned.

"Those tending the pigs ran off and reported this in the town and countryside, and the people went out to see what had happened. When they came to Jesus, they saw the man who had been possessed by the legion of demons, sitting there, dressed and in his right mind; and they were afraid. Those who had seen it told the people what had happened to the demon-possessed man — and told about the pigs as well. Then the people began to plead with Jesus to leave their region.

"As Jesus was getting into the boat, the man who had been demon-possessed begged to go with him. Jesus did not let him, but said, 'Go home to your family and tell them how much the Lord has done for you, and how He has had mercy on you.' So the man went away and began to tell in the Decapolis how much Jesus had done for him. And all the people were amazed."

What actions characterized this man?

_____

_____

_____

How would you like this guy living next door? Or institutionalized nearby?

Did Jesus fear this man? ❏ Yes ❏ No
Did Jesus care about him? ❏ Yes ❏ No

What was Jesus willing to sacrifice for this man? (verses 11-13)

_____

_____

What was the result for this man? (verse 15)

_____

_____

Did the town people think the pigs were worth the man? (verses 15-17)

_____

_____

Why do you think they send Jesus away?

_____

_____

_____

Would you say these people were in their "right minds"?

_____

_____

Are you in your right mind? Check yourself: I sometimes . . .

- . . . do self-destructive things ❑
- . . . drive people away from me ❑
- . . . allow evil things in my life ❑
- . . . think things are more valuable than people ❑
- . . . fear Jesus ❑
- . . . send Jesus away ❑

What would be the qualities of a person in his right mind, found by Jesus?

PRAYER:
Father, am I in my right mind? Am I found by your Son, Jesus?

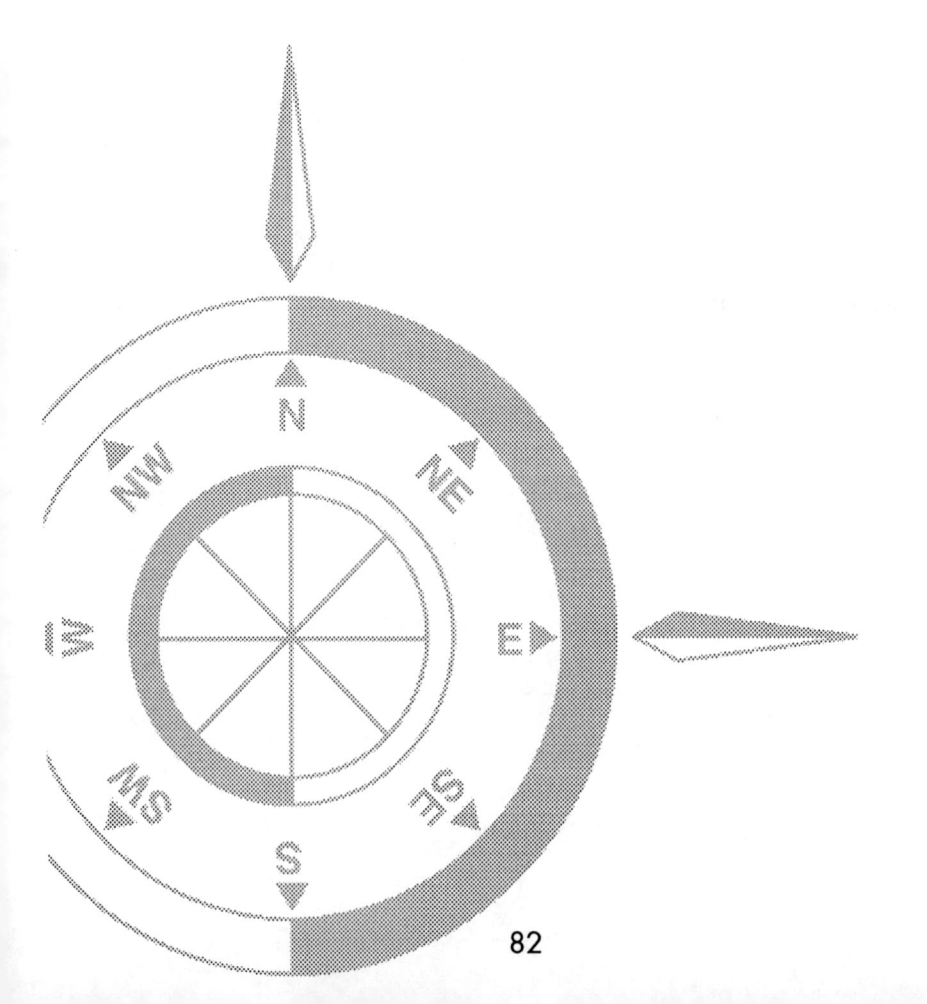

WEEK 8
HAVING IT ALL
Jesus Came to Give Abundant Life

Pretend it's your birthday. What would you like to have?

A home computer? A sport coat? Automatic dishwasher? Diamond ring? Name something.

Of all the things in the world, why do you want this thing? Do you think you'll get it?

When we are children, we generally want toys, games, toy guns, surprises.

When we become adults, we still want toys! Only they are bigger and more expensive than ever! But we also begin to long and wish, more and more, for other gifts, the intangible, increasingly invaluable presents: peace of mind, quiet joy, good relationships, meaning to life's madness.

Jesus came bearing gifts. Not big-screen TVs or mink coats. He brought *real* gifts: the kind of gifts that satisfy our longings for more than a week; the kind that don't need a warranty against breakage; the kind that are stored in the heart rather than in the closet.

"I have come that they may have life, and have it to the full."

But even gifts don't leap into your lap, open themselves up and put themselves to work making your life better.

Gifts must be unwrapped. Directions read. Some assembly may be required. New clothes washed and ironed. And EVERY GIFT must be accepted, then utilized, or it's just a white elephant.

Have you received Jesus' gift, the abundant life? If not, open it this week, using the scissors of this Bible study!

MONDAY

FOCUS:
Lord Jesus, you made quite a trip in order to give me the abundant life. Show me how I can better accept this gift this week for Your glory. Amen.

Your "truest love" is Jesus Christ. "I have loved you with an everlasting love," says Jeremiah 31:3. Will you accept the gift He has had for you from the beginning?

Even since then, He has wanted you to have this gift, the gift of the great life. The abundant life. The alive life. The truly good life. The life intended from the beginning.

If someone had this life, how do you think they would act, think, walk, talk?

_____
_____
_____

Jesus obviously had this full life — that's the only way He could give it. Scan through as much of Luke's gospel as you have time, beginning with chapter 5, answering this question: What was Jesus like?

_____
_____
_____
_____
_____

Based on what you just wrote, where would your abundant life tank read:

___ Empty   ___ ¼   ___ ½   ___ ¾   ___ Full

PRAYER:
Lord, make me like You!

TUESDAY

Why was Jesus so full of the abundant life? It was not simply because He was God's Son. Daily stress, discomfort, hardship and hunger were still a part of His life, and even more so than in ours. He lived in a third-world society, remember, the kind we only experience on short-term mission trips (and then with plenty of American money for protection).

And then there was the cross. That was no luxury cruise!

Why was Jesus confident when others were afraid? Peaceful when everyone else was anxious? Patient when people were angry? Caring when the crowd was apathetic? Powerful when the rest were weak?

What clues do you pick up from Jesus' early life in Luke 2:41-52?

"Every year his parents went to Jerusalem for the Feast of the Passover. When he was twelve years old, they went up to the Feast, according to the custom. After the Feast was over, while his parents were returning home, the boy Jesus stayed behind in Jerusalem, but they were unaware of it. Thinking he was in their company, they traveled on for a day. Then they began looking for him among their relatives and friends. When they did not find him, they went back to Jerusalem to look for him. After three days they found him in the temple courts, sitting among the teachers, listening to them and asking them questions. Everyone who heard him was amazed at his understanding and his answers. When his parents saw him, they were astonished. His mother said to him, 'Son, why have you treated us like this? Your father and I have been anxiously searching for you.'

"'Why were you searching for me?' he asked. 'Didn't you know I had to be in my Father's house?' But they did not understand what he was saying to them.

"Then he went down to Nazareth with them and was obedient to them. But his mother treasured all these things in her heart. And Jesus grew in wisdom and stature, and in favor with God and men."

_____

_____

When you go out of town for a convention or vacation, where do you usually visit? What are you interested in doing or seeing?

___ beach sunning   ___ eating out

___ mall shopping   ___ golfing
___ sight-seeing   ___ other

Do you expect these things to give you satisfaction and joy? Why? Why do you look to events, externals, extras to give you the good life rather than your relationship with God?

Do you skip church when on a trip? Do you take your Bible? Do you spend less time in prayer? Do you think more about the fun than God? Do you pray about your trip in advance?

Who was anxious in Luke 2:41-52? _____ Are you anxious or can you peacefully say verse 49?

PRAYER:
With God, evaluate your last out-of-town trip. Get His perspective on it.

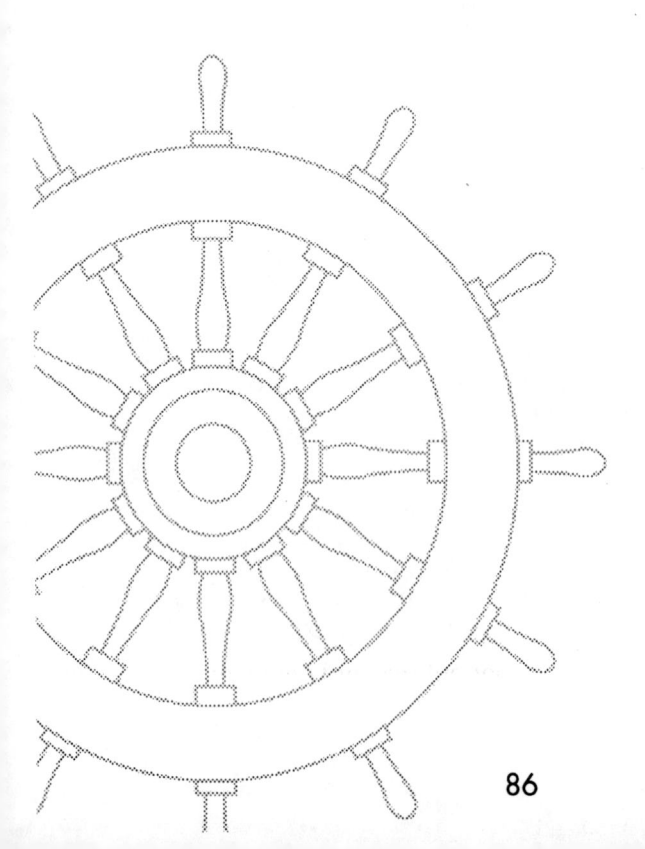

WEDNESDAY

FOCUS:
Rather than praying for yourself, pray for others. Rather than asking for things, give thanks.

Eve's words to God in the garden were, "The serpent deceived me, and I ate."

We, too, can be deceived, and eat of things we should not eat. Or be deceived and expect what we eat to satisfy what only God can satisfy. Or be deceived and eat too much of what is good, so we don't have an appetite for what is best.

Satan wants us living on baloney. Seeking junk food rather than real nourishment. Buying "food that will not satisfy" (Isaiah 55:2). When you eat too much baloney, even steak may not be appealing.

List the three temptations in Luke 4:1-15, and how Jesus answered each:
"Jesus, full of the Holy Spirit, returned from the Jordan and was led by the Spirit in the desert, where for forty days he was tempted by the devil. He ate nothing during those days, and at the end of them he was hungry.
"The devil said to him, 'If you are the Son of God, tell this stone to become bread.'
"Jesus answered, 'It is written: "Man does not live on bread alone."'
"The devil led him up to a high place and showed him in an instant all the kingdoms of the world. And he said to him, 'I will give you all their authority and splendor, for it has been given to me, and I can give it to anyone I want to. So if you worship me, it will all be yours.'
"Jesus answered, 'It is written: "Worship the Lord your God and serve him only."'
"The devil led him to Jerusalem and had him stand on the highest point of the temple. 'If you are the Son of God,' he said, 'throw yourself down from here. For it is written: "He will command his angels concerning you to guard you carefully; they will lift you up in their hands, so that you will not strike your foot against a stone."'
"Jesus answered, 'It says: "Do not put the Lord your God to the test."'

"When the devil had finished all this tempting, he left him until an opportune time.

"Jesus returned to Galilee in the power of the Spirit, and news about him spread through the whole countryside. He taught in their synagogues, and everyone praised him."

1. _____
   _____
2. _____
   _____
3. _____
   _____

What do you hunger for? What do you catch yourself secretly longing for, thinking "if only I had more _____ then I'd be happy."

   ___ power, position   ___ financial security
   ___ prestige   ___ a life mate, closer family
   ___ physical comfort   ___ to do something great
   ___ other _____

Which of Jesus' three answers do you need to give to your hunger today? Circle it.

Will you, like Jesus, stand on God's word and sufficiency? You see the results in verse 14.

PRAYER:
Give your answer to God.

THURSDAY

FOCUS:
How did you satisfy your hungers yesterday?
Let God show you where He filled you.
Let Him show you where you tried to fill yourself.

How do you sleep? Do you drop right off? Do you toss and turn? Are your dreams peaceful? Do you wake up refreshed?

My sleep is _____

_____

What do you worry about most?

- ❏ money
- ❏ sin in your life
- ❏ health
- ❏ nameless worry
- ❏ kids
- ❏ doing things right
- ❏ business success
- ❏ other

Read Luke 8:22-25 and write below what stands out to you in this story.
    "One day Jesus said to his disciples, 'Let's go over to the other side of the lake.' So they got into a boat and set out. As they sailed, he fell asleep. A squall came down on the lake, so that the boat was being swamped, and they were in great danger. The disciples went and woke Him, saying, 'Master, Master, we're going to drown!' He got up and rebuked the wind and the raging waters; the storm subsided, and all was calm. 'Where is your faith?' he asked his disciples. In fear and amazement they asked one another, 'Who is this? He commands even the winds and the water, and they obey him.'"

_____

_____

_____

About what in your life is Jesus saying, "Where is your faith?"

_____

_____

_____

Can Jesus tame what you are losing sleep over? Look at another escapade at sea in Matthew 14:22-36. Why did Peter fall?

"Immediately Jesus made the disciples get into the boat and go on ahead of him to the other side, while he dismissed the crowd. After he had dismissed them, he went up on a mountainside by himself to pray. When evening came, he was there alone, but the boat was already a considerable distance from land, buffeted by the waves because the wind was against it.

"During the fourth watch of the night Jesus went out to them, walking on the lake. When the disciples saw him walking on the lake, they were terrified. 'It's a ghost,' they said, and cried out in fear. But Jesus immediately said to them: 'Take courage! It is I. Don't be afraid.' 'Lord, if it's you,' Peter replied, 'tell me to come to you on the water.' 'Come,' he said. Then Peter got down out of the boat, walked on the water and came toward Jesus. But when he saw the wind, he was afraid and, beginning to sink, cried out, 'Lord, save me!' Immediately Jesus reached out his hand and caught him. 'You of little faith,' he said, 'why did you doubt?' And when they climbed into the boat, the wind died down. Then those who were in the boat worshiped him, saying, 'Truly you are the Son of God.'

"When they had crossed over, they landed at Gennesaret. And when the men of that place recognized Jesus, they sent word to all the surrounding country. People brought all their sick to him and begged him to let the sick just touch the edge of his cloak, and all who touched him were healed.'"

What crisis have you had just lately? _____

Where were your eyes focused during that crisis?

___ Jesus   ___ Me   ___ Circumstances

Look at how Jesus spent the evening before this episode (verse 23). How do you usually spend your evenings?

What do you usually do right before going to bed? What will you change, based on today's study?

PRAYER:
Confess to God.

FRIDAY

FOCUS:
Help me decide today, Lord, if I am willing to pay the price for the abundant life.

What do you learn about the "hows" and "whys" of Jesus' actions and life from John 5:17-30?

"Jesus said to [the Jews], 'My Father is always at his work to this very day, and I, too, am working.' For this reason the Jews tried all the harder to kill him; not only was he breaking the Sabbath, but he was even calling God his own Father, making himself equal with God.

"Jesus gave them this answer: 'I tell you the truth, the Son can do nothing by himself; he can do only what he sees his Father doing, because whatever the Father does the Son also does. For the Father loves the Son and shows him all he does. Yes, to your amazement he will show him even greater things than these. For just as the Father raises the dead and gives them life, even so the Son gives life to whom he is pleased to give it. Moreover, the Father judges no one, but has entrusted all judgment to the Son, that all may honor the Son just as they honor the Father. He who does not honor the Son does not honor the Father, who sent him.

"'I tell you the truth, whoever hears my word and believes him who sent me has eternal life and will not be condemned; he has crossed over from death to life. I tell you the truth, a time is coming and has now come when the dead will hear the voice of the Son of God and those who hear will live. For as the Father has life in himself, so he has granted the Son to have life in himself. And he has given him authority to judge because he is the Son of Man.

"'Do not be amazed at this, for a time is coming when all who are in their graves will hear his voice and come out — those who have done good will rise to live, and those who have done evil will rise to be condemned. By myself I can do nothing; I judge only as I hear, and my judgment is just, for I seek not to please myself but him who sent me.'"

Hows: _____
_____
_____
_____

Whys: _____
_____
_____
_____

Jesus only did what He saw His Father doing, what the Father led Him to do. "I do not seek my own will, but the will of him who sent me." How much can the son do on His own? (verse 19)

_____

How much can you do on your own? (John 15:5)

_____

What did Jesus say we must do to gain life in Matthew 16:24-26?
- ☞ deny _____
- ☞ take up your _____
- ☞ follow _____
- ☞ lose your _____ for my sake.

What are you clinging to that blocks the word and life of God in your life? Bitterness toward an enemy? Illicit sex life? Precious personal time? Hoarding money? Protecting a day off? Your night out? Getting your will for your life?

[   ]

Go back to John 5 and try to say Jesus' words of verses 17, 19 and 30, but for yourself. Can you? What must change in your life to say them?

PRAYER:
To have Jesus' life in you, you must let go of your desperate graspings for life and fulfillment, and say, "Thy will be done, Thy life come . . . into me!"

WEEK 9
HIDE AND SEEK
Jesus Came to Light the Darkness

Have you ever been afraid of the dark? Did you ever lie awake at night as a child, afraid to hang your arm over the bedside for fear of a monster reaching out from under the bed and getting you?

Have you ever watched a horror movie, become frightened, and turned on a light, just to feel safer?

Did you ever walk home at night and begin to get that creepy feeling of being followed, then begin walking faster and faster until you suddenly bolted for the door, to arrive panting with your heart racing?

The dark can do funny things to even the most stalwart of hearts. In the dark you can't see where you are going or what might be waiting for you there. In the dark, you are easily tricked. A shadow becomes a goblin. In the dark, you are more likely to be hurt, tripping over a table, bumping into a corner. In the dark, you are more likely to be robbed, molested, or mugged.

Satan is called "the prince of darkness." He wants you in darkness: fear-driven, sweaty-palmed, confused, seeing what's not really there, bumping into obstacles, robbed of joy and light.

2 Corinthians 4:4 says "The god of this age has blinded the minds of unbelievers, so that they cannot see the light of the gospel."

Are you still afraid of the dark? You needn't be. Verse 6 says, "For God, who said, 'Let light shine out of darkness,' made his light shine in our hearts to give us the light."

Put a lamp to your dark places this week, the lamp of God's Word.

MONDAY

FOCUS:
Are you willing to allow God to shine His spotlight on any and every part of your life? Pray about it.

Don't you love Christmas lights? Well, at least most Christmas lights. There are those gaudy, mix and match displays. But we like most lights because they shine out against the black darkness and bring cheer and hope. Today, we study the Christmas light.

Isaiah 9:1-7 contains one of the great prophecies. Read the passage, highlighting what stands out to you.

"Nevertheless, there will be no more gloom for those who were in distress. In the past he humbled the land of Zebulun and the land of Naphtali, but in the future he will honor Galilee of the Gentiles, by the way of the sea, along the Jordan — The people walking in darkness have seen a great light; on those living in the land of the shadow of death a light has dawned. You have enlarged the nation and increased their joy; they rejoice before you as people rejoice at the harvest, as men rejoice when dividing the plunder. For as in the day of Midian's defeat, you have shattered the yoke that burdens them, the bar across their shoulders, the rod of their oppressor. Every warrior's boot used in battle and every garment rolled in blood will be destined for burning, will be fuel for the fire. For to us a child is born, to us a son is given, and the government will be on his shoulders. And he will be called Wonderful Counselor, Mighty God, Everlasting Father, Prince of Peace. Of the increase of his government and peace there will be no end. He will reign on David's throne and over his kingdom, establishing and upholding it with justice and righteousness from that time on and forever. The zeal of the Lord Almighty will accomplish this."

Are there any ways in which you feel you are "walking in darkness?" (verse 2) These prompters may help you:

I worry about _____

_____

I am addicted to _____

_____

I am confused about _____

_____

I continue to stumble and sin by _____

_____

Who or what are you relying on to shed light on your problems?

_____

What are we specifically promised in verses 3 and 4?
"enlarged the _____"
"increased the _____"
"shattered the _____"

(Circle) the promise from Scripture that you most need today in your life. How will these promises be accomplished, according to the last line of our passage?

_____

How much do you believe God's zeal and the gift of Jesus are sufficient to handle your problems?

110%   90%   60%   35%   10%   0%

How much does God want your darkness lit up?

110%   90%   60%   35%   10%   0%

PRAYER:
Ask God to light your dark places today. What does He show you about them?

95

TUESDAY

FOCUS:
"If I say, 'Surely the darkness will hide me, and the light be night around me,' even the darkness will not be dark to you; the night will shine like the day, for darkness is as light to you" (Psalm 139:11-12).

Go again to Isaiah 9:1-7. See if you can find three reasons that show this passage is referring to Jesus.

"Nevertheless, there will be no more gloom for those who were in distress. In the past he humbled the land of Zebulum and the land of Naphtali, but in the future, he will honor Galilee of the Gentiles, by the way of the sea, along the Jordan — The people walking in darkness have seen a great light; on those living in the land of the shadow of death a light has dawned. You have enlarged the nation and increased their joy; they rejoice before you as people rejoice at the harvest, as men rejoice when dividing the plunder. For as in the day of Midian's defeat, you have shattered the yoke that burdens them, the bar across their shoulders, the rod of their oppressor. Every warrior's boot used in battle and every garment rolled in blood will be destined for burning, will be fuel for the fire. For to us a child is born, to us a son is given, and the government will be on his shoulders. And he will be called Wonderful Counselor, Mighty God, Everlasting Father, Prince of Peace. Of the increase of his government and peace there will be no end. He will reign on David's throne and over his kingdom, establishing and upholding it with justice and righteousness from that time on and forever. The zeal for the Lord Almighty will accomplish this."

1. _____
2. _____
3. _____

If you need help, here are three:

Verses 1-2 = Matthew 4:12-16

"When Jesus heard that John had been put in prison, he returned to Galilee. Leaving Nazareth, he went and lived in Capernaum, which was by the lake in the area of Zebulun and Naphtali — to fulfill what was said through the prophet Isaiah: 'Land of Zebulun and land of Naphtali, the way to the sea, along the Jordan, Galilee of the Gentiles — the people living in darkness have seen a great light; on those living in the land of the shadow of death a light has dawned.'"

Verse 6 = Matthew 1:23
"'The virgin will be with child and will give birth to a son, and they will call him Immanuel' — which means, 'God with us.'"

Verse 7 = Matthew 1:1
"A record of the genealogy of Jesus Christ the son of David, the son of Abraham."

List the four names Jesus is given in verse 6:
1. _____
2. _____
3. _____
4. _____

Of the four names, which has come to be the most meaningful to you?
_____

Why did you choose this one? _____
_____

Which name has the least personal significance? _____
Why?_____

Which name is most needed to apply to your area of darkness from yesterday's lesson?
_____

Choose one of the four names of Jesus which you want to know in a fuller, more real way: _____

PRAYER:
Ask God to show you how trusting this name of Jesus can change your life today! Prayerfully read the reference that applies to the name you have chosen.

Wonderful Counselor: *Matthew 6*

Mighty God: *John 20*

Everlasting Father: *John 14:1-14*

Prince of Peace: *Matthew 11:28-30, Luke 2:1-30*

WEDNESDAY

FOCUS:
Think back about the name of Jesus you prayed about yesterday. Can you see a way God made that truth about Jesus come more alive yesterday? (Note: it may not have been a dramatic revelation. God often works through the very simplest of things.)

How much do you think you have life figured out? Mark an 'X' on the graph.

|—————————————————|
All   Most   Some   Little   None

What do you usually do when God tells you to do something that makes absolutely no sense to you?

    a) reject it; it can't be His will
    b) wait; see if He keeps telling me
    c) argue; show God why it can't work
    d) do it and eagerly anticipate seeing God do something outside my experience

Read Matthew 1:18-25 and write anything said or done that would have seemed awfully unusual to Joseph.

    "This is how the birth of Jesus Christ came about: His mother Mary was pledged to be married to Joseph, but before they came together, she was found to be with child through the Holy Spirit. Because Joseph her husband was a righteous man and did not want to expose her to public disgrace, he had in mind to divorce her quietly.

    "But after he had considered this, an angel of the Lord appeared to him in a dream and said, 'Joseph son of David, do not be afraid to take Mary home as your wife, because what is conceived in her is from the Holy Spirit. She will give birth to a son, and you are to give him the name Jesus, because he will save his people from their sins.'

    "All this took place to fulfill what the Lord had said through the prophet: 'The virgin will be with child and will give birth to a son, and they will call him Immanuel' — which means, 'God with us.'

    "When Joseph woke up, he did what the angel of the Lord had commanded him and took Mary home as his wife. But he had no union with her until she gave birth to a son. And he gave him the name Jesus."

_____

_____

If you had been Joseph, what would have been your emotions, fears, and thoughts in marrying an already pregnant woman, and becoming surrogate father to this special child?

_____

_____

_____

Do you think Joseph felt adequate for the task? _____

Which of the four choices above regarding God's will was Joseph's choice?
    a) ❑   b) ❑   c) ❑   d) ❑

Which of the four choices would have been yours? More realistically, which of the choices is yours today? More than likely, God is already asking you to do something that goes against your plan and thinking. Prayerfully ask God if there is something He is telling you that appears to contradict common sense, goes against your desires, or seems above your strength? What is it? Will you do it? Write out your thoughts below.

THURSDAY

FOCUS:
How desperate are you for light, for truth, for revelation?

Read Matthew 2:1-12 and note what the Magi must go through in order to find and worship the King.

"After Jesus was born in Bethlehem in Judea, during the time of King Herod, Magi from the east came to Jerusalem and asked, 'Where is the one who has been born king of the Jews? We saw his star in the east and have come to worship him.'

"When King Herod heard this he was disturbed, and all Jerusalem with him. When he had called together all the people's chief priests and teachers of the law, he asked them where the Christ was to be born. 'In Bethlehem in Judea,' they replied, 'for this is what the prophet has written: "But you, Bethlehem, in the land of Judah, are by no means least among the rulers of Judah; for out of you will come a ruler who will be the shepherd of my people Israel."'

"Then Herod called the Magi secretly and found out from them the exact time the star had appeared. He sent them to Bethlehem and said, 'Go and make a careful search for the child. As soon as you find him, report to me, so that I too may go and worship him.'

"After they had heard the king, they went on their way, and the star they had seen in the east went ahead of them until it stopped over the place where the child was. When they saw the star, they were overjoyed. On coming to the house, they saw the child with his mother Mary, and they bowed down and worshiped him. Then they opened their treasures and presented him with gifts of gold and of incense and of myrrh. And having been warned in a dream not to go back to Herod, they returned to their country by another route."

_____
_____
_____

The Magi went to great lengths to follow the star of Bethlehem. They traveled several hundred miles to see the Light. How far would you be willing to travel to know Jesus better:

❏ 3,000 miles ❏ 500 miles ❏ 50 miles ❏ 10 miles ❏ 1 mile?

The Magi's journey was one of several weeks, even months. How much time would you be willing to give to meet Jesus in a deeper way:
❏ 5 minutes ❏ 30 minutes ❏ 1 hour ❏ 10 hours
❏ 1 week ❏ 1 month ❏ 1 year?

List the things you currently do to know the Light, Jesus Christ, better?
_____
_____
_____

What were the Magi's motives for finding Jesus? (verse 2)
_____

Herod's motive was far less noble, and he didn't get to see Jesus. How noble is your motive for knowing Jesus? Which statement is truest for you? "My motive for seeking Jesus is to:

    ___ worship Him better."
    ___ relieve my nagging guilt."
    ___ answer all my questions."
    ___ be happy."
    ___ do something for Him."
    ___ feel better."

Read verses 10 and 11 again. How can you follow the example of the Magi this season?
_____
_____

PRAYER:
Worship Jesus the Light.

FRIDAY

FOCUS:
Worship Jesus again to begin your time today.

As you worshiped today and yesterday, did you sense more light, peace, confidence, joy in your life, or the same, or less?

❏ more   ❏ same   ❏ less

Write everything said about the light in John 1:1-9.

"In the beginning was the Word, and the Word was with God, and the Word was God. He was with God in the beginning. Through him all things were made; without him nothing was made that has been made. In him was life, and that life was the light of men. The light shines in the darkness, but the darkness has not understood it. There came a man who was sent from God; his name was John. He came as a witness to testify concerning that light, so that through him all men might believe. He himself was not the light; he came only as a witness to the light. The true light that gives light to every man was coming into the world."

_____

_____

_____

Notice that Jesus is the light. Rewrite John 8:12 here:

_____

_____

_____

Underline what we must do to avoid walking in darkness. What keeps people from walking in the light? Read John 3:19-21.

"This is the verdict: Light has come into the world, but men loved darkness instead of light because their deeds were evil. Everyone who does evil hates the light, and will not come into the light for fear that his deeds will be exposed. But whoever lives by the truth comes into the light, so that it may be seen plainly that what he has done has been done through God."

Is there anything in your life that you would not want exposed for everyone to see?

___

Will you hold it up to the light of Jesus and see it for what it is? Will you hate it and despise it as a sick and ugly thing, and repent of it?

The man who doesn't mind his deeds being exposed knows those deeds have been really done by whom? (verse 21)

___

What important role do we now play and who should get the glory for it? Read Matthew 5:14-16.

"You are the light of the world. A city on a hill cannot be hidden. Neither do people light a lamp and put it under a bowl. Instead they put it on its stand, and it gives light to everyone in the house. In the same way, let your light shine before men, that they may see your good deeds and praise your Father in heaven."

___

Write "Jesus Christ" on a sheet of paper and put it in your pocket as a reminder today that He is with you every minute as your strength, your love, your guide, your light. Walk with Him, and worship Him! "Oh come, let us adore Him, Christ the Lord!"

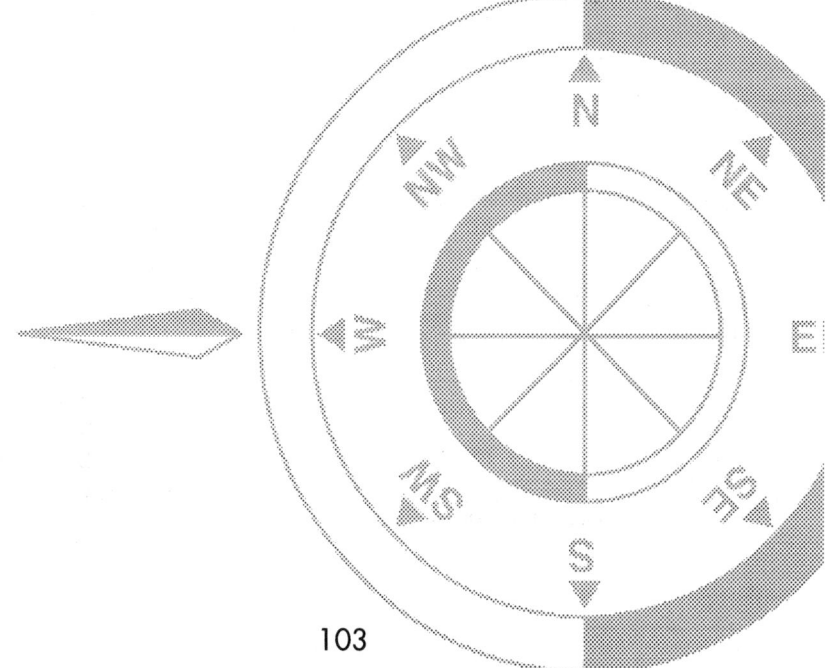

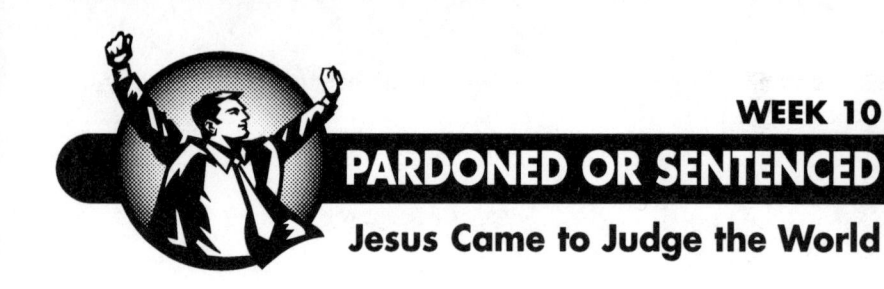

WEEK 10
PARDONED OR SENTENCED
Jesus Came to Judge the World

"Here cum da judge!"

We don't hear much about judgment, but we should be exceedingly glad that Jesus came to judge the world. Let's look at just what is emphasized at the holidays and why.

People love baby stuff. When you see an infant, what do you say? "Coochie-coo, oh, how cute" and such things, no matter how homely the tot may be. A sweet, innocent baby in a rough manger pulls at heartstrings. Throw in angels singing, shepherds watching, wise men with shower gifts, and that's the stuff of Christmas!

We love babies because babies are not threatening. They never talk back (at least not in language we can understand). They don't correct us or challenge us. They don't *judge* us like grown-up people do.

Have you ever wondered why Christmas is so much bigger than Easter? No one strings lights for Easter. Schools don't break two weeks. Companies don't have office Easter parties. No store advertises "just eight more shopping days till Easter!"

Why? Because Jesus in a manger is more palatable than Christ on a cross. He's not so "coochie-coo sweet" as the exalted, resurrected Lord. Christmas calls for a holiday spirit; the cross calls for the Holy Spirit. At Christmas, the Salvation Army rings for pocket change; at Easter, God rings for life change. The manger moves us to sing carols; the empty tomb demands a pledge of allegiance.

Jesus equals judgment. He didn't come for the cradle, but the cross and the throne. And all who stand in His way will be judged. That's good news when you are standing behind Him rather than standing up to Him.

MONDAY

FOCUS:
Father, this week, teach us new truth regarding Jesus and His role as Judge.

Here are several character qualities. When you think of Jesus, which do you think of most often? ✓ Check them.

___ Loving	___ Kind
___ Teaching	___ Praying
___ Healing	___ Judging
___ Angry	___ Patient
___ Holy	___ Almighty

(Circle) those you *often* think of when you think of *God*.

✶ Star those qualities above that you would consider negative characteristics.

Are Jesus and God any different?
   ___Yes   ___No

Is any one quality of God/Jesus less important than another? Example: Is God more loving than He is righteous?
   ___Yes   ___No

If you are in the right, do you want a wise, just judge to decide your case?
   ___Yes   ___No

If, as a child, you were being abused, would you want your father to get angry and do something about it?
   ___Yes   ___No

You see, a judge is not a bad person, unless you are a criminal. Anger is not a bad quality if the anger is in a powerful friend and directed toward your enemy.

All of God's qualities are Jesus' qualities, and all their qualities are good — if you are on their side!

Are you on Jesus' side?
          ___Yes   ___No

Where do you see judgment in Luke 1:46-55 and 2:21-35, and is it positive or negative?

"And Mary said: 'My soul glorifies the Lord and my spirit rejoices in God my Savior, for he has been mindful of the humble state of his servant. From now on all generations will call me blessed, for the Mighty One has done great things for me — holy is his name. His mercy extends to those who fear him, from generation to generation. He has performed mighty deeds with his arm; he has scattered those who are proud in their inmost thoughts. He has brought down rulers from their thrones but has lifted up the humble. He has filled the hungry with good things but has sent the rich away empty. He has helped his servant Israel, remembering to be merciful to Abraham and his descendants forever, even as he said to our fathers.'"

"On the eighth day, when it was time to circumcise him, he was named Jesus, the name the angel had given him before he had been conceived.

"When the time of their purification according to the Law of Moses had been completed, Joseph and Mary took him to Jerusalem to present him to the Lord (as it is written in the Law of the Lord, 'Every firstborn male is to be consecrated to the Lord'), and to offer a sacrifice in keeping with what is said in the Law of the Lord: 'a pair of doves or two young pigeons.'

"Now there was a man in Jerusalem called Simeon, who was righteous and devout. He was waiting for the consolation of Israel, and the Holy Spirit was upon him. It had been revealed to him by the Holy Spirit that he would not die before he had seen the Lord's Christ. Moved by the Spirit, he went into the temple courts. When the parents brought in the child Jesus to do for him what the custom of the Law required, Simeon took him in his arms and praised God, saying: 'Sovereign Lord, as you have promised, you now dismiss your servant in peace. For my eyes have seen your salvation, which you have prepared in the sight of all people, a light for revelation to the Gentiles and for glory to your people Israel.'

"The child's father and mother marveled at what was said about him. Then Simeon blessed them and said to Mary, his mother: 'This child is destined to cause the falling and rising of many in Israel, and to be a sign that will be spoken against, so that the thoughts of many hearts will be revealed. And a sword will pierce your own soul too.'"

PRAYER:
God, show me that no title Jesus bears is a bad title, no name a negative name, no work an unnecessary work. Jesus is just as much judge as Savior. Help us to see His judging role in a new light, and worship Him.

TUESDAY

FOCUS:
Would you rather pray to a righteous, just God or a prejudiced, selfish god?
What will you say to God about His righteousness?

What do you learn about Jesus as judge in John 3:16-21?

"For God so loved the world that he gave his one and only Son, that whoever believes in him shall not perish but have eternal life. For God did not send his Son into the world to condemn the world, but to save the world through him. Whoever believes in him is not condemned, but whoever does not believe stands condemned already because he has not believed in the name of God's one and only Son. This is the verdict: Light has come into the world, but men loved darkness instead of light because their deeds were evil. Everyone who does evil hates the light, and will not come into the light for fear that his deeds will be exposed. But whoever lives by the truth comes into the light, so that it may be seen plainly that what he has done has been done through God."

_____
_____
_____

And in John 5:24-30?

"I tell you the truth, whoever hears my word and believes him who sent me has eternal life and will not be condemned; he has crossed over from death to life. I tell you the truth, a time is coming and has now come when the dead will hear the voice of the Son of God and those who hear will live. For as the Father has life in himself, so he has granted the Son to have life in himself. And he has given him authority to judge because he is the Son of Man. Do not be amazed at this, for a time is coming when all who are in their graves will hear his voice and come out — those who have done good will rise to live, and those who have done evil will rise to be condemned. By myself I can do nothing; I judge only as I hear, and my judgment is just, for I seek not to please myself but him who sent me."

_____
_____
_____

Jesus does not have to actively judge. That is, He does not have to investigate and determine who is in and who is out. He knows all. Those who accept Him and His truth are in, for He is the only way. Those who reject Him or try to make it on their own or merely give Christ lip service have judged themselves, condemned themselves.

1 Corinthians 11:31 says, "If we judged ourselves, we would not come under judgment." Examine yourself. What areas of your life are surrendered to Jesus and His control? Put a + on each one.

Choice of friends	Free time
Career future	Sex life
Prayer life	TV life
Right to retaliate	Finances
Sins of the past	Ego

What are you currently doing that you know comes under His judgment, yet you continue anyway? Ask God to show you.

These things are not going to be judged by Jesus; they already are judged and condemned. Will you change? Who would benefit most from your change?

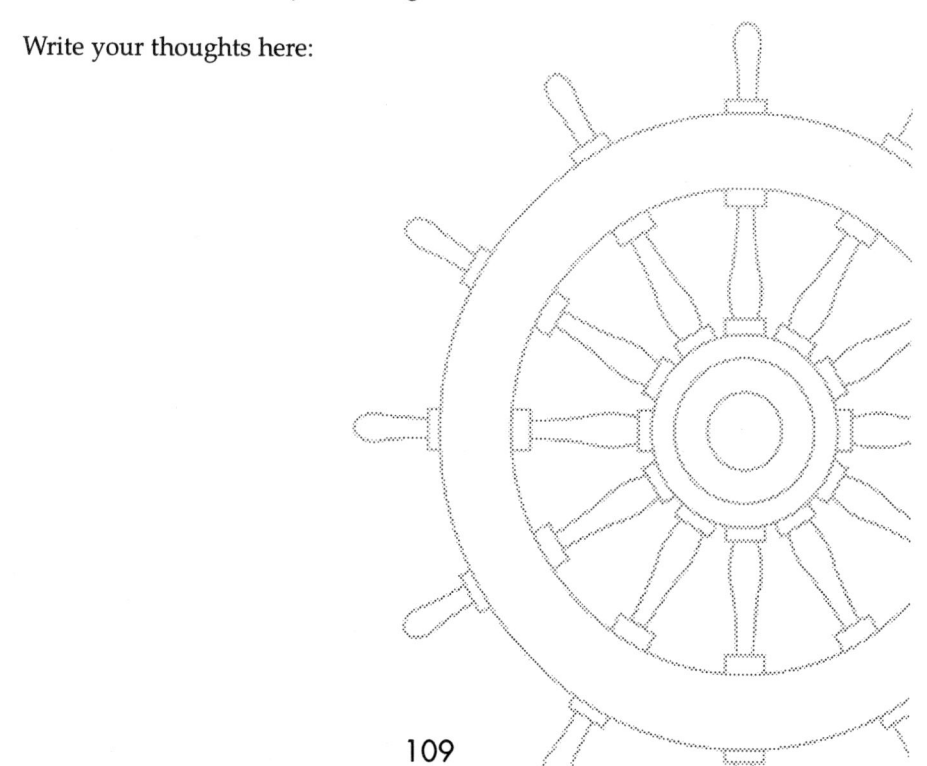

Write your thoughts here:

WEDNESDAY

FOCUS:
Show me, Lord Jesus, was I any different yesterday?

Underline God's purpose in judging us in 1 Corinthians 11:32.
"When we are judged by the Lord, we are being disciplined so that we will not be condemned with the world."

All of God's judgments rendered before the "Final Judgment" while we are still on earth are God's spurs in our ribs, meant to change our course. Jesus told Paul, "It is hard for you to kick against the goads."

Write three things the Bible says about God's discipline in Hebrews 12:5-11.
"And you have forgotten that word of encouragement that addresses you as sons: 'My son, do not make light of the Lord's discipline, and do not lose heart when he rebukes you, because the Lord disciplines those he loves, and he punishes everyone he accepts as a son.' Endure hardship as discipline; God is treating you as sons. For what son is not disciplined by his father? If you are not disciplined (and everyone undergoes discipline), then you are illegitimate children and not true sons. Moreover, we have all had human fathers who disciplined us and we respected them for it. How much more should we submit to the Father of our spirits and live! Our fathers disciplined us for a little while as they thought best; but God disciplines us for our good, that we may share in his holiness. No discipline seems pleasant at the time, but painful. Later on, however, it produces a harvest of righteousness and peace for those who have been trained by it."

1. _____
2. _____
3. _____

Describe how you were disciplined as a child.

_____
_____
_____

How have (do, will) you disciplined your children?

_____

_____

What is your usual reason for disciplining your kids?

_____

_____

What is always God's reason for disciplining? (verses 6,10)

_____

_____

What does God's discipline prove about you? (verses 7, 8)

_____

_____

Is there a time in your past when you felt God was severely disciplining you? Describe it.

_____

_____

How do you feel about that discipline now? Underline one: regretful, appreciative, bitter, relieved?

PRAYER:
Are there any areas where you see God disciplining you now?
❏ No
❏ Yes. Here's how:

THURSDAY

FOCUS:
God wants fingertip control of your life. Reflect on yesterday. Did He have that?

Today we come to a very relieving and freeing lesson! The fact that Jesus is judge does have its advantages.

First, we must ask: Who have you allowed to pass judgments on you? On a separate sheet of paper, consider each relationship listed below, and note any area in which they still control or condemn you. Do this prayerfully. For some, this may be fearful, but remember Who is with you.

- Mother and father
- Each brother and sister
- Current or former spouse
- Each of your children
- Closest friend
- Boss/company
- Society/culture/media (example: "success is a large house with a two-car garage, or having a great figure, etc.")

What does the apostle Paul say about human judgments in 1 Corinthians 4:1-5?

"So then, men ought to regard us as servants of Christ and as those entrusted with the secret things of God. Now it is required that those who have been given a trust must prove faithful. I care very little if I am judged by you or by any human court; indeed, I do not even judge myself. My conscience is clear, but that does not make me innocent. It is the Lord who judges me. Therefore, judge nothing before the appointed time; wait till the Lord comes. He will bring to light what is hidden in darkness and will expose the motives of men's hearts. At that time each will receive his praise from God."

Verse 3 says, "I do not even judge _____ ." Do you allow your judgments to get in the way of the Lord's? Do you condemn yourself when He pardons you? Do you excuse actions He despises? What are you hardest on yourself about? Name three things you most often criticize about yourself:

1. _____
2. _____
3. _____

Circle the judgments that come from God; "X" those that come from your own weak conscience or are passed down from one of the people listed above.

Who do you really want to judge you? An imperfect parent? A fallible friend? A mixed-up you? Or the Lord Jesus who always judges rightly and with compassion.

PRAYER:
Jesus, I want you to have the sole judgeship of my life.

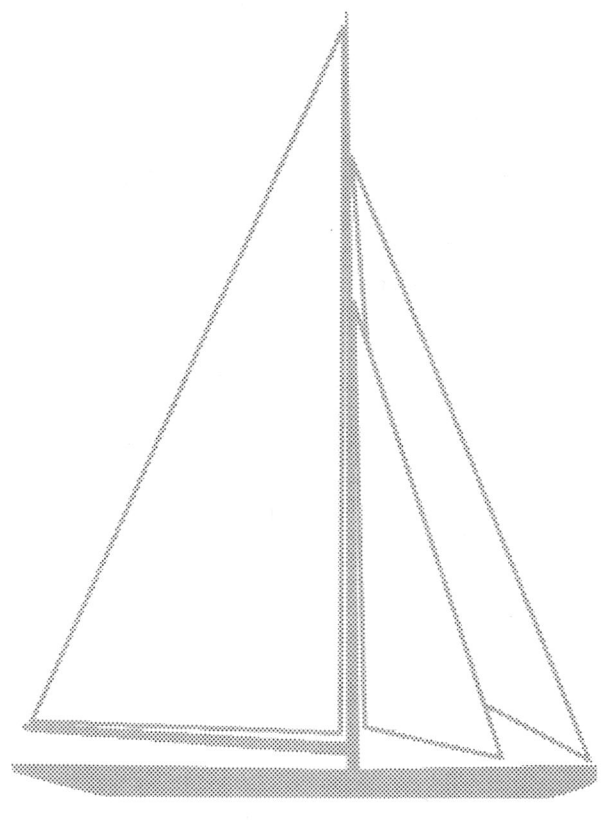

FRIDAY

FOCUS:
How different could your life be if Jesus was your sole judge? How would it feel to have one judge, not one hundred judges, trying to tell you how to live your life? Ask God to reveal this to you before your study time today.

Today we have an equally freeing truth. Rewrite Jesus' words from Matthew 7:1-2 in your own words.

"Do not judge, or you too will be judged. For in the same way you judge others, you will be judged, and with the measure you use, it will be measured to you."

_____

_____

_____

Yesterday, you looked at several relationships and tried to determine if you were allowing people to judge you. Get another sheet of paper and determine whether you judge any of those same people! Do you make value judgments on what they do? Do you honor them less than you should because they don't meet your standards? Do you spend more energy loving them or re-engineering them? Think through each one!

If verse 2 is true, then what will be the criteria by which Jesus will judge you?

_____

How do you feel about that?

_____

_____

What will you do to change it?

_____

Picture your life free of evaluating others, clear of criticizing, absent of nitpicking. How much more energy would you have to love?

      Same   10%   25%   50%   75%   100%

Would you be happier or sadder? Would others be happier or sadder?

"Who are you to judge someone else's servant? To his own master he stands or falls. And he will stand, for the Lord is able to make him stand" (Romans 14:4).

PRAYER:
Free me, Lord Jesus!

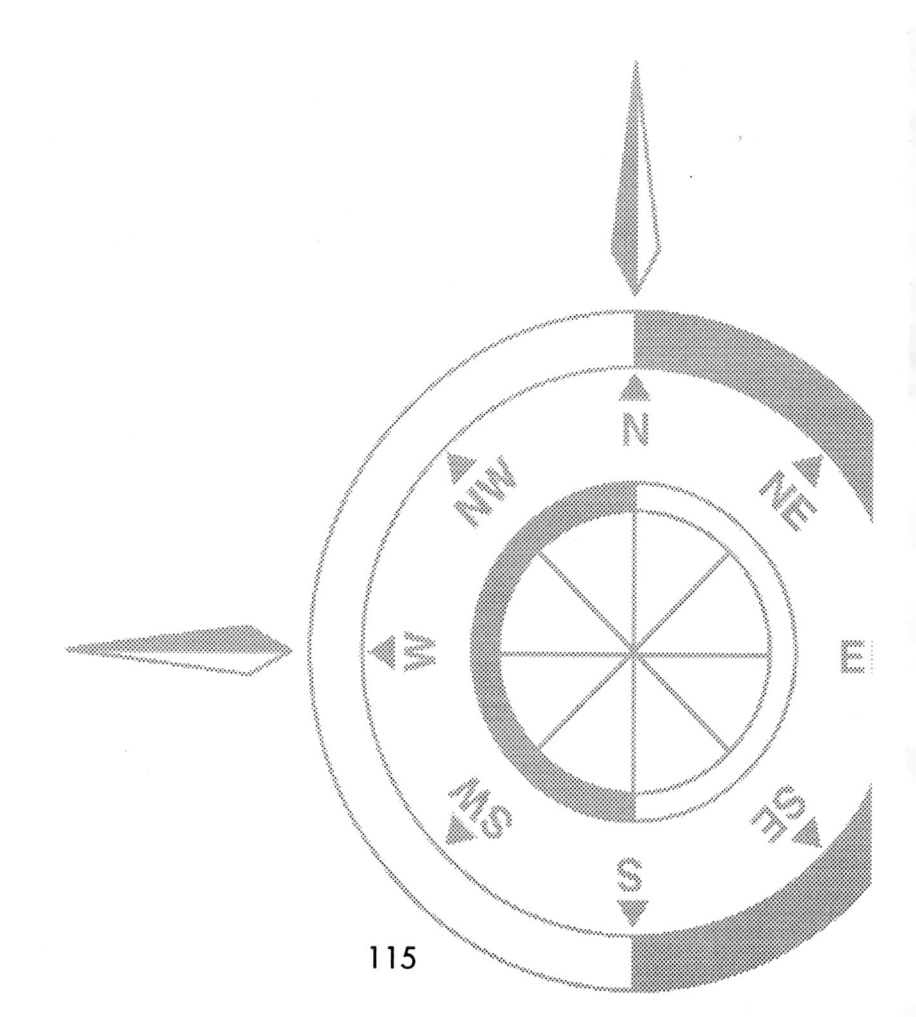